TEACHING AND LEARNING IN THE INTERMEDIATE MULTIAGE CLASSROOM

Alice Leeds
David Marshak

A SCARECROWEDUCATION BOOK

The Scarecrow Press, Inc.
Lanham, Maryland, and London
2002

A SCARECROWEDUCATION BOOK

Published in the United States of America
by Scarecrow Press, Inc.
A Member of the Rowman & Littlefield Publishing Group
4720 Boston Way, Lanham, Maryland 20706
www.scarecroweducation.com

4 Pleydell Gardens, Folkestone
Kent CT20 2DN, England

British Library Cataloguing in Publication Information Available

Library of Congress Cataloging-in-Publication Data

Leeds, Alice.
  Teaching and learning in the intermediate multiage classroom / Alice Leeds,
David Marshak.
    p. cm.
  Includes bibliographical references and index.
  ISBN 0-8108-4399-4 (alk. paper)—ISBN 0-8108-4278-5 (pbk. : alk. paper)
    1. Nongraded schools. I. Marshak, David. II. Title.

LB1029.N6 L38 2002
372.12'55—dc21   2002019805

This book is dedicated to Alice's parents, Goldye and Woody Leeds, whose love of learning inspires her still; and to Noorjehan Sarah Johnson, who first taught David about the value of multiage classrooms from the child's perspective.

CONTENTS

PART II: THE BENEFITS OF THE MULTIAGE
CLASSROOM

PART III: SUCCEEDING AT MULTIAGE TEACHING

ACKNOWLEDGMENTS

Alice Leeds thanks Jane Maisel for detailed and insightful feedback on the first draft; my students and colleagues at Lincoln Community School, the Montessori Children's House of Durham, and the Montessori Family School of Manhattan for providing years of shared adventures in learning as well as rich fodder for this project; my sisters—and fellow teachers—Robin Drogin and Marcy Leeds for their willingness to serve as my sounding boards; my husband, Rick Ceballos, for his willingness to serve me delicious meals throughout this project; and the many teachers who helped me arrive at this time and place.

David Marshak thanks the multiage teachers in Addison Northeast Supervisory Union in Vermont (John Bourgoin, Debbie Cross, Carol Hasson, Jodi Lane, Pat Minor, and Arnell Paquette), John Richardson, the principal at Sunnyslope Community School, and the Sunnyslope multiage teachers (Vicki Voorhees, Kelly Best, Diana Holmlund, Cathy Hulet, Tom LaFerriere, Dave Matheny, Ginny Semler, Debbie Snowden, Sharon Tankersley, Stacey Stands, and Mary Jo Porter) for teaching him about the nature and value of multiage classrooms.

Alice and David both thank Janet Banks and Russell Yates for their insightful review of the manuscript and their encouraging comments, and Tom Koerner for his interest in and support of this project.

INTRODUCTION

It is our conviction that multiage elementary classrooms can provide children, their teachers, and their parents with a better form of education than can be offered within age-graded, conventional classrooms. Multiage elementary classrooms are better in terms of personal and social growth and development, and better in terms of both conventional academic achievement and self-motivated and self-directed learning. Even in this era of state-mandated academic standards and high-stakes testing, in many states teachers can continue to draw upon the benefits of multiage structures as they help their students:

- learn how to learn effectively;
- pursue their own curiosity, interests, and passions;
- become skilled at communicating and working with others;
- gain the values and skills essential to acting as responsible citizens in a democracy;
- prepare to score adequately on state-mandated tests; and
- prepare for academic and personal success in secondary school and in adult life.

We believe that all of these outcomes can be accomplished simultaneously and integrally, in an effectively structured and enacted multiage classroom.

This book focuses on the schooling of children who would be in the intermediate grades in a conventional school: grades 3 or 4 through grades 5 or 6, ages eight or nine through twelve or thirteen. Most of the books about multiage classrooms published in the past decade have described practices for students in the primary grades: kindergarten through grades 2 or 3. The intent of this book is twofold:

- to offer a detailed example and discussion of one multiage teaching practice in an intermediate multiage classroom to interested teachers, administrators, and parents;
- to provide these readers with pertinent information about four related topics: the personal and social benefits of multiage classrooms for children, teachers, and parents; the academic benefits of multiage classrooms; the relationships between multiage academics and state-mandated standards and tests; and the process of becoming a multiage teacher.

In part 1 of this book, Alice Leeds, who has taught multiage grades 4/5/6 or 5/6 in a Vermont public school for twelve years after devoting seven years to teaching primary grade multiage classes, describes how her classroom functions and how she has organized the various multiage elements within her class structure, curriculum, instruction, and assessment. Leeds provides a detailed set of insights about how an intermediate multiage classroom works effectively, day to day, month to month, and year to year.

In parts 2 and 3 of this volume, David Marshak, a teacher-educator who has studied multiage classrooms for fourteen years, explores the four related topics noted previously. Leeds concludes the book with chapter 13.

* * *

We are convinced that the multiage classroom is much more than a different way of grouping children in school. In its effective realization, as described in a number of teacher-written books from the 1990s—for example, *Exploring the Multiage Classroom* by Anne Bingham, with Peggy Dorta, Molly McClaskey, and Justine O'Keefe (Stenhouse, 1995); *Full Circle: A New Look at Multiage Education* by Penelle Chase and Jane Doan (Heinemann, 1994); *A Multiage Classroom: Choice and Possibility* by Maureen McCann Miletta (Heinemann, 1996); *Creating the Multiage Classroom* by Janet Caudill Banks (CATS Publications, 1995); *A Room with a Different View* by Jill Ostrow (Stenhouse, 1995); and *Cre-*

ating Nongraded K–3 Classrooms: Teachers' Stories and Lessons Learned edited by Ric Hovda, Diane Kyle, and Ellen McIntyre (Corwin Press, 1996)—the multiage classroom is a different and better way to organize school for the vast majority of children. The practice of age grading labels and limits many children, promotes destructive forms of competition, restricts collaboration, and inhibits social relationships with children other than one's age peers. It also pushes teachers to "teach to the middle," and it wastefully discards relationships between teachers and children—and teachers and parents—every June.

In contrast, multiage classrooms promote acceptance and the valuing of children's diverse qualities and capabilities, foster both collaboration and healthy competition, and encourage relationships between younger and older children. They push teachers to provide appropriate instruction and learning opportunities for individual learners, and they draw advantage from the relationships among teachers, students, and parents over two or more years.

Multiage classrooms are both based upon and promote the following qualities and principles.

Personalization   Every child is valued. Every child deserves a high-quality education. Every child needs to learn how to think, communicate, and learn. Multiage teachers know that children grow in unique and personal ways, that children at the same chronological age are likely to have greatly varied needs and capacities, that children learn in many different ways, and that children have passionate interests and curiosities. Multiage teachers know that part of their responsibility is to personalize each child's education and that their success in this endeavor can result only from their knowledge of each child as an individual, their caring about each child, and their relationship with each child over several years. Multiage teachers know that part of their work is to guide each child's learning and growth.

Building Community   Multiage classrooms are communities that include children and their teacher(s) and, to a significant extent, the children's parents or guardians. This community takes an active role in educating and supporting children.

Valuing Both Standard Knowledge and Personal Knowledge   Multiage teachers value *standard knowledge* when the academic standards include a reasonable mix of concepts, facts, and skills. A number of states have adopted such balanced standards. Multiage teachers also value *personal knowledge*, meaning both the understandings and knowings that children create through their engagement with their own interests and questions—and the self-awareness, self-understanding, and interpersonal qualities and skills that children develop through their exploration of these interests. In multiage classrooms, teachers guide children to integrate standard knowledge with personal knowledge. Both are acknowledged and valued. Neither is set in conflict against the other.

In multiage classrooms, children construct much of the knowledge. But much standard knowledge is also transmitted to children or discovered by children. The interests, passions, and curiosities of children in such classrooms help shape the curriculum, as do the state's and local district's academic standards.

Using Social Interaction to Promote Learning   As Charles Rathbone noted in *Multiage Portraits: Teaching and Learning in Mixed-Age Classrooms* (Crystal Springs Books, 1993, pp. 154–157), multiage classrooms provide all of the elements that Lev Vygotsky described as necessary for the use of social interaction to promote learning: the presence of an adult or more capable peer; social interaction between the learner and the adult or more capable peer; the enactment of the interaction in language comprehensible to both persons; and the necessity that the adult or more capable peer operate in the learner's "zone of proximal development," defined as the intellectual territory between the child's current intellectual abilities on her/his own and the higher level of abilities the child can achieve through a collaborative and/or guiding interaction with an adult or more capable peer.

In multiage classrooms, children do work and learn on their own. But just as often or perhaps more often, they work and learn with other children—their colleagues—and with their teacher. These children have the freedom to seek out other children who can help them operate in their personal zone of proximal development in a particular learning situation. Children combine and recombine continuously throughout the day, accessing again and again their zone of proximal development. Children learn at their own pace, so at each new level of knowledge and complexity, they have a new zone of proximal development and can find new colleagues who can help them—and whom they can help.

Vygotsky wrote, "All the higher mental functions originate as actual relations between people."[1] In multiage classrooms, children are continually engaged in relating—and learning.

Nurturing Resilience   Resilient children overcome the difficulties and wounds in their childhood to become healthy and successful adults. They are not unalterably impaired by adversity; rather, they find ways to make their lives work for them. One definition of "resilience" is "the capacity to spring back, rebound, successfully adapt in the face of adversity, and develop social, academic, and vocational competence despite exposure to severe stress or simply to the stress that is inherent in today's world."[2]

Bonnie Benard has identified four traits that are common in resilient children and adults: social competence and relationship skills; problem-solving skills; autonomy (i.e., a sense of oneself and the ability to act independently); and a sense of purpose in one's life.[3] Each of these traits is invited and nurtured in the daily life of multiage classrooms.

Nan Henderson and Mike Milstein have described six strategies that can promote resiliency in children, the first three from the research of J. D. Hawkins and Richard Catalano[4] and the next three from Benard's synthesis of pertinent studies.[5]

1. *Increase bonding.* "[C]hildren with strong positive bonds (to adults, peers, and activities) are far less involved in risk behaviors than children without these bonds."[6] Multiage classrooms promote bonding through their multiyear duration, the ways in which children teach and learn from one another, the lessening of peer competition in comparison with single-grade classes and the corresponding increase in collaboration, and the enhanced opportunities for children to explore their interests and passions.

2. *Set clear and consistent boundaries.* Given the social complexity of multiage classrooms and the relative freedom and responsibility that children have to organize their own use of time, multiage classrooms demand clear, consistent boundaries for children's behavior. Multiage teachers usually engage their students in helping to articulate the boundaries, and children in multiage classrooms usually help maintain respect for these boundaries among their peers.

3. *Teach life skills.* These include cooperation skills, communication skills, problem-solving skills, conflict-resolution skills, and decision-making skills. Considering the centrality and intensity of social interaction in multiage classrooms, these life skills are also inevitably central to the curriculum. Teachers provide instruction

and modeling in these skills, and so do peers, particular "elder" students in the classroom who "own" the norms and help maintain them. Additionally, children in many multiage classrooms learn to make decisions regularly about how to use their time and how to conduct their learning and schoolwork.

4. *Provide caring and support.* The emotional core of multiage classrooms is the enhanced caring and support that come both from the teacher and from peers as a result of the multiyear relationships, the heightened commitments of such relations, and the natural stewardship that older children accept for younger peers in a classroom community.

5. *Set and communicate high expectations.* Since teachers in multiage classrooms know their students very well by the start of each child's second year in the classroom, teachers can more readily set high yet attainable expectations for every child. Teachers can also help children articulate high yet realistic expectations for themselves.

6. *Provide opportunities for meaningful participation.* Such opportunities include involving children in making decisions about the rules in their classroom and about what they study. Again, multiage classrooms are defined in their essence by the ongoing opportunity for children to participate in learning and classroom life in ways that children help create and thus experience as meaningful.

In sum, multiage classrooms embody all of the characteristics that the foremost researchers and advocates of promoting resiliency in children have identified as central to this end.

Promoting Collaboration   Multiage classrooms are profoundly collaborative. Children learn from one another as well as from the teacher. Teachers learn from their students. Teachers and parents work together in a more connected way than in most single-grade classrooms. And most multiage teachers work collaboratively with other multiage teachers, either in the classroom itself via teaming or outside the classroom in relation to curriculum planning, problem solving, and mutual support.

Encouraging Reflection and Professional Learning and Innovation Multiage teachers reflect on their teaching, and they are carried into ongoing innovation by their commitments to children as individuals and by their own curiosity as learners. Children are encouraged to pursue their own interests, so multiage teachers must scramble to support their students' inquiries. They learn from their students as well as teach them. Multiage teachers rarely complete a multiyear cycle of curriculum and choose to repeat exactly what they have just done. Rather, they seek new, better ways of integrating students' personal learning with the standards-based learning of the required curriculum.

All of the qualities and principles noted above are evident both in the chapters written by Alice Leeds and in the voices of the many other multiage teachers who speak about their work in this book.

NOTES

1. L. S. Vygotsky, *Mind in Society* (Cambridge, Mass.: Harvard University Press, 1978), p. 57.

2. N. Henderson and M. Milstein, *Resiliency in Schools: Making It Happen for Students and Educators* (Thousand Oaks, Calif.: Corwin Press, 1996), p. 7.

3. B. Benard, "Fostering Resiliency in Urban Schools," in B. Williams, ed., *Closing the Achievement Gap. A Vision for Changing Beliefs and Practices* (Alexandria, Va.: Association for Supervision and Curriculum Development, 1996), p. 99.

4. J. D. Hawkins and R. F. Catalano, *20 Questions: Adolescent Substance Abuse Risk Factors* (Seattle, Wash.: Developmental Research and Programs, Inc., 1990), audiotape.

5. B. Benard, *Fostering Resiliency in Kids: Protective Factors in the Family, School, and Community* (Portland, Oreg.: Northwest Educational Lab, 1991).

6. Henderson and Milstein, *Resiliency in Schools*, p. 12.

I

TEACHING AND LEARNING IN THE INTERMEDIATE MULTIAGE CLASSROOM

1

THE LINCOLN
COMMUNITY SCHOOL

Six miles up from Bristol along the Lincoln Gap Road is a one-story wooden structure painted barn red with crisp white trim. A crisply painted wooden sign on this building introduces it as the Lincoln Community School. Behind the school, the New Haven River rushes by as it scurries down from Mount Abraham, a lofty peak that looks down on us as we go about our days. Our intermediate students and teachers hike the two miles up to Mount Abe's steep summit each fall as an opening ritual to the school year. Winters are long in Lincoln, Vermont, a small mountain town about forty miles southeast of Burlington. The mountain's first snow falls in October, so we must schedule our hike early. Each year we ponder the idea of returning to Mount Abe's summit in the spring, but winter lingers in Vermont well into April, followed by a season of thick mud, which oozes around our shoes and tires and finally surrenders to summer sometime in June. So we never quite make the return trip as a bookend to our school year. Instead, we take an easy streamside walk in which students can get as wet and muddy as they please without worrying about slipping off a high ledge.

Notwithstanding the harsh winter, our school has an idyllic setting that is well appreciated by the Lincoln community, a combination of native Vermonters and transplants. While Lincoln, like Vermont in general, lacks the cultural diversity found in much of our United States, it does have its own sort of variety. Those who have chosen Lincoln as their home—including artists, writers, and entrepreneurs—are generally distinct from community members who have lived in Vermont for generations. Lincoln's strong Christian community likewise contrasts with families who associate with other paths, such as the local Native American/Tibetan Buddhist retreat. These differences influence what people want and expect in the education of their children; community members have strongly held contrasting views, which they express freely at school board sessions and annual town meetings. Debates over arts integration, basic skills, and cooperative learning are not uncommon. And perhaps because we are a small community, each voice is usually heard.

Our five-town school district includes an elementary school in each town and a single-campus middle school and high school, Mt. Abraham Union. Collaboration among educators from each district school is ongoing in relation to issues such as portfolio assessment, curriculum development, and multiage networking. Our district curriculum coordinator works with teachers and administrators to create annual in-service days that bring staff from the town schools together. Teachers across our district most frequently interact with one another at district-sponsored graduate classes offered on-site at the high school.

Yet in many important ways, our little school is largely self-directed. Lincoln Community School, with approximately 120 students, is the smallest school in our district. We also enjoy small class sizes, typically ranging from twenty to twenty-four students. In recent years, the community and the school board have been carefully generous with school budgets, and we are frequent recipients of grant funding; these grants have helped compensate for the limited cultural and educational resources available in a small rural setting. Also of great benefit are the many community members who share their talents and skills at our annual Lincoln Community Days, a several-day period when local painters, naturalists, musicians, writers, potters, geologists, and maple sugar tappers instruct our students and help us celebrate the subtle signs of spring. Although most parents work outside of town, they try to offer their time and support in classrooms, at fund-raisers, and during school functions. Burlington, one hour away, is the closest cultural center, and many classes schedule field trips there several times each year.

Our school has an unusual history in regard to our multiage classrooms. Unlike many schools that initiate multiage in the primary grades, the multiage approach at Lincoln received broader support from the outset at the intermediate level, where it has now been in place for fifteen years. Six years ago, in response to concerns and questions from the community, a team of parents and teachers set out to evaluate our multiage program. The results were a glowing endorsement of our intermediate multiage approach. Nevertheless, our primary grades—which are collaborating on a wonderful Reading Recovery Program—have not fully embraced the multiage philosophy. As a staff, we have learned to operate cohesively and supportively even though we do not always share the same educational approaches.

I arrived at Lincoln Community School nine years ago with seven years' experience as a Montessori teacher, during which time I had worked in multiage primary programs in New York City and in Durham, North Carolina. During my first five years at Lincoln, my grades 4/5/6 class teamed with an adjacent 4/5/6 class. For the past four years, I've had a 5/6 classroom. Because we are so small, a shift in the school population can have dramatic impact on class size; the last year that we had two 4/5/6 classes, they contained half the population of our entire school. We reconfigured into one 5/6 and one 4/5/6 combination for one year in order to maintain small class sizes throughout the school. Then we moved into our current structure of two 5/6 classes.

When changes of this kind are proposed, our staff meets to consider their effects on students. And even though—perhaps because—we are small, the diversity of philosophies among our staff and community requires us all to work together with open-mindedness and sensitivity. The success of our intermediate multiage program can be documented by the fact that it has continued to exist and to prosper through many challenging times. Our responsiveness to the changing needs of students and our community makes for a vital program. During the course of writing this book, our multiage program has altered its configuration, its curriculum, and its assessment practices, yet we remain steady in our central beliefs about how children learn and how multiage programs can support the learning process.

2

ACADEMIC DEVELOPMENT IN THE INTERMEDIATE MULTIAGE CLASSROOM

"**T**oday, as a continuation of our study of rockets, you will work in pairs to design and build a balloon-powered rocket car," I explain to my fifth- and sixth-grade class, revealing the car I built over the weekend to focus attention. "You will have the entire day without interruption to work on this project."

At this, a murmur spreads across the room.

"Your challenge is to design a car with the most thrust, or power."

I intentionally do not give a more specific definition of the best out-come; I want the students to make some decisions about this on their own.

"First, design your car on graph paper with the materials I will make available. Next, construct your car. Be sure to follow safety guidelines. After your cars are constructed, you will conduct test runs in the multi-purpose room. We will share our data on a group chart, which will also have space for your comments. I encourage you to share ideas and make adaptations to your design as you go along. Finally, you will submit a math portfolio write-up of your solution and your conclusions about the design features of an ideal rocket car. Incorporate the rate formula and what you know about Newton's third law."

At this point, I ask students to restate the directions briefly to a part-ner, and then I have a few volunteers review them for the whole group.

"Your work will be scored according to math portfolio criteria"— the Vermont Math Portfolio is a rubric-based assessment tool—"so remember to use good communication and problem-solving skills. You need not have the most successful car to receive a top score."

After a quick demonstration of Lynx™ safety tools and materials, I present each student with a slender dowel, a stick of wood, and some cardboard triangular joiners. Immediately, everyone is engaged. With a blend of care and enthusiasm, students measure their materials and begin drawing plans on graph paper. Some exchange and discuss ideas as they go along, while others are caught up in their own internal dialogues.

Toward the end of the morning, students are completing their cars and preparing for test runs. Each student pair anchors a flexible straw to their car, places a balloon on one end of the straw, and inflates the balloon by blowing through the other end. There is a burst of enthusiasm as each car takes off. If it doesn't, there is a slight groan followed by a consultation between the architects. Adjustments are then made to the angle in the elbow of the straw, to the position at which the straw is anchored, or to the overall design.

Student pairs gather yardsticks, measuring tape, calculators, and stopwatches and head for the multipurpose room. They begin to record distance, duration, and rate of speed of their cars, along with the inflated balloon's circumference and the car's dimensions. When a car has a particularly good run, students gather around and discuss the reasons for this success. Before long, students are exchanging their attractive wooden wheels for the much lighter and simpler cardboard varieties, thus lightening their payloads. Some students are quietly discovering the optimal positioning of their straws. Still others are dismantling their cars and sawing them down to a smaller size. As the data grow, patterns emerge, and students begin to see what factors result in an ideal balloon-powered rocket car.

So what identifies this classroom description as a multiage classroom? Although it is clear that some students grasp the parameters of this task more readily or more fully than others, it is difficult to separate students by age or grade level as they go about their work. It is evident, however, that they have come to know and respect one another's areas of expertise. One fifth grader is particularly adept at using the stopwatch, while another has caught on quickly to the use of Lynx tools. A sixth grader plans a wisely designed slender car model that seems to travel a leap beyond the others. Sometimes students discover one another's talents by surprise, and then they become incorporated into the group knowledge base, without any regard for grade levels.

This classroom looks much like any other in which students are challenged by exciting multisensory and discovery-based learning opportunities. Nonetheless, there is a special quality to this classroom that derives from its multiage character. In this classroom, students learn and achieve without limitations from age grading or age-based expectations. The nature and depth of relationships that develop over a multiyear period among a group of mixed-age students and their teacher(s) provide opportunities for learning and accomplishment that cannot exist in single-grade classrooms. And every school year "veteran" students return to the multiage classroom and carry forward the learning and accomplishments from the previous year through an evolving classroom culture.

STRUCTURED FREEDOM: CREATIVITY WITHIN CHALLENGING GUIDELINES

As have all other states, Vermont has adopted a new set of academic standards, the Framework of Standards and Learning Opportunities. Our vision is "high skills for every student, no exceptions, no excuses." Interestingly, this move toward increased academic expectations for all students has resulted in the need for more creativity and freedom in the development of exciting, challenging, and relevant curriculum materials. Vermont's new academic standards place increased emphasis on problem solving, communication skills, and integration across subject areas, as well as incorporating a renewed emphasis on the arts.

I believe that multiage classrooms can help students achieve these standards—and often exceed them—by engaging students in conditions of structured freedom. With this intent, I present my students with many projects that have defined goals *and* room for individual creativity. I am up front with them about the big picture, the learning outcomes or targets I have in mind for them. In designing their balloon-powered rocket cars, for example, students worked within clearly defined scientific and mathematical guidelines. Simultaneously, they had significant freedom in terms of how they conducted themselves, and so they felt empowered and engaged as they designed and built their cars. One sixth-grade female student remarked, "This is the best day of my life!" Interestingly enough, the most stringent parameters in this activity were the physical principles that the students discovered in the process of carrying out the task.

As an aside, I want to point out the value of projects such as the "Rocket Car Challenge" in which students are given an entire day to produce a product. I have offered whole-day projects such as this on several occasions, both with small groups of students and with the whole class, and the results are consistently positive. Students thank me for allowing them the time to put so much effort into a single project. Even the students who complete their work quickly soon realize how much further they could go, and before long, they return to their work with new ideas for embellishments and improvements. No time is lost in picking up and taking out work, and students have plenty of time to share and develop their insights. The faculty and administration at my school have been graciously tolerant of my periodic requests to pull our class out of the schedule grid for a day. One year the entire staff got excited about this idea and planned a free day into the calendar each month. (I personally find it works best to create these days when the time is ripe for it.) When ample time is provided for a challenging and creative project, students relish the opportunity as much as they do an exciting field trip. The results I have seen with such projects prove to me an understanding often overlooked in instructional planning: given engaging and age-appropriate tasks with plenty of time to carry them out, young people can display a lengthy attention span.

MULTIYEAR PLAN

Because a curriculum of structured freedom is our chosen approach, our multiage curriculum requires a multiyear plan. For math, this is a fairly straightforward affair, since our school uses a sequential, ability-based math curriculum. In our intermediate classrooms, language arts are quite naturally integrated with social studies, so we have one set of multiyear units for those two combined subjects. Science also requires a multiyear sequence of units tied to state and national standards, and these units are closely linked with math concepts. In addition to the close pairing of language arts/social studies and math/science, we reach for cross-curricular connections across all subjects, and language arts skills are in constant use across the curriculum. At least once each year, we carry a unit fully across the curriculum, honoring the integrity of each subject area. An example of this sort of integration is offered in chapter 8, which describes our homes unit.

Although it is certainly not ideal for the continuity of a multiage program, we occasionally reconfigure our grade-level combinations or shuffle several students to maintain small class sizes of fewer than twenty-five students, allowing us to individualize according to student needs. (In our small school of seven classrooms, a population bulge for a given age level can throw off the entire distribution of students.) When moving a particular student, we choose one who we feel could benefit from a switch. Because of this possibility, we have found it important to coordinate our curriculum sequence as a whole school. Then, if the need to make a change arises, the curriculum will remain consistent for each child.

Once curriculum topics or categories are clear, we look for interesting ways to meld them into a unified multiyear program. Because our program was for many years a grades 4/5/6 model, we initially prepared a three-year plan designed for our trimester grading system. This plan, based broadly on the Montessori elementary curriculum, is illustrated below. As our outline shows, we begin each school year with a unit that integrates fully across the curriculum, and we also try to maintain an overall theme for each school year. One of the nice things about a rotating curriculum plan is that older students get their younger peers excited about upcoming topics. For example, our unit on Greek mythology has always been popular with students, and incoming students frequently ask about it when they arrive in our class.

We change and adapt units—and even the big picture—as curriculum guidelines and educational research change, though, and sometimes we need to drop a unit while adding one that we feel would be valuable to our students. This can sometimes produce a snowball effect. Our school is currently revising our approach to science in response to new national and state standards in this area. We recently decided as a whole school to emphasize specific science standards each year. As a result, our space unit has become a cross-disciplinary unit on flight that encompasses the physics, chemistry, biology, history, and social impact of this topic. Needless to say, our entire multiyear sequence has been impacted by this change.

Although we may schedule the same unit topic in a subsequent multiyear plan, an individual unit is never repeated in the same way that it was previously undertaken, because we develop new aspects and minimize or omit others. A couple of years ago, we paired our familiar Greek studies unit with a poetry writing unit for the first time. Students wrote poems about mythological characters using several different poetic devices. But we also had to play down our Greek festival because of other competing events that particular year.

* *

THREE-YEAR UNIT PLAN

Year 1   **OUR UNIVERSE, OUR PLANET**
Space: Astronomy, Rocketry, and Science Fiction (cross-disciplinary)
Geology (cross-disciplinary)
Life on Earth: Botany and Ecosystems (cross-disciplinary)

Year 2   **DEVELOPMENT OF HUMAN CULTURE**
Home, Architecture, and Structure (cross-disciplinary)
The Renaissance (language arts/social studies emphasis)
Electricity (math/science emphasis)
Greek Mythology (language arts/social studies emphasis)
Inventions (math/science emphasis)

Year 3   **THE U.S. AND OUR PLACE IN THE SCHEME OF THINGS**
Passing the Word Along: Arriving at Twentieth-Century Communication (cross-disciplinary)
American History (language arts/social studies emphasis)
Human Body/Sound (math/science emphasis)
American Geography (language arts/social studies emphasis)
Wildlife in America (math/science emphasis)

* *

INTEGRATED UNITS

As a Montessori elementary teacher, I was introduced early on to the concept of curriculum integration. In what are known as "cultural studies," we broadly considered the history of scientific ideas and the evolution of cultures, and math was integrated with history and science through mathematical folktales and problem solving. When I began working with intermediate-grade students, the need for more rigorous concept and skill development necessitated an approach that assured a deeper and more specific level of understanding. I began to look at integration in a new light.

I now strive to present opportunities in which students develop both a sense of the big picture and a clear understanding of the parts of the whole. This is an ongoing challenge, one that is addressed with great inspiration in Project 2061, the science standards developed by the Association for the Advancement of Science. This project has created a vision for presenting rigorous science standards strongly tied to math and technology curricula and also paired with the humanities. Along with my colleagues, I eagerly look toward the development of an array of curricular materials that meet these lofty standards across the curriculum. Meanwhile, I try to use the best materials available to develop exciting units that maintain curricular integrity within each subject area addressed.

High-level integration occurs most readily within the previously stated pairings of math/science and language arts/social studies. Sometimes, as in my Montessori experiences referred to above, a history or geography topic will also lead to a math portfolio problem or a class reading will relate to a science theme. For example, while studying ancient Greek mythology, the students compared the usability of the Greek and Roman number systems in a problem-solving activity. Likewise, our weekly student newspaper (*TIME for Kids*) often includes articles on scientific developments relevant to our unit of study in science. These articles provide the opportunity to discuss science topics from a social studies perspective—the impact of current research on modern society, the culture of science, or the long-term benefits of medical discoveries. Increasingly, the best-prepared curriculum materials consider these sorts of connections in a sophisticated and developmentally appropriate context.

At least once each year, we plan a unit that integrates richly across the curriculum. Our space unit, for example, addresses rocketry, the space program in the context of modern history, astronomy, mythology of the constellations, electronic space art and music, image processing, and science fiction.

TEAM TEACHING

Although I am currently teaching all subject areas, for most of the past seven years, I shared classroom responsibilities with a job-share partner with whom I collaborated closely. Prior to that time—and again currently—I teamed with the intermediate teacher in an adjoining classroom. In all these cases, two teachers created exciting cross-disciplinary units by sharing the load. Even when using well-prepared teacher resource materials, social studies and science in particular require extensive planning at the intermediate level, so each teacher can take responsibility for planning and/or presenting one of those areas or for an aspect of a given unit. The result is a richer classroom program than could be planned by either teacher alone. Another benefit of sharing across classrooms is that curricular resources go twice as far, and each classroom benefits from double its budgetary allotment.

CULMINATING EVENTS

Each unit concludes with a special event or product. This might be a performance, a presentation, a publication, an exhibit of student work, or any combination of these. The broad possibilities provided by these projects make them work well in a multiage setting, where each student's work can be adapted to his or her level of ability and interest.

In a unit on Greek mythology, after working on a series of cooperative activities relating to the myths, student groups each planned a final creative project related to a subtopic of interest. Groups worked on puppet shows, murals, dramatic presentations, newspapers, and news reports. (These activities and culminating events are detailed in an *Interact* unit called "Odyssey.") As a class, we also worked on movement collages that portrayed some of the myths. These, along with the students' poems, were presented during a Greek festival.

Our space unit ended with a celebration in which we blasted off a number of different kinds of rockets, both commercial models and student designs. One of the rockets was caught in a tall tree on its descent, and students still reminisced about this unit almost two years later when they peered out the window on a winter day to see "Brian's rocket" peeking through the branches.

A class publication is a great way to share the writing program with parents. Each year our class publishes a collection of student work that is shared with parents and sometimes sold as a fund-raising effort for our spring field trip. Students will cherish these booklets in years to come, and parents have the opportunity to view their child's writing in the context of a spectrum of student writing.

Our unit on homes, described in chapter 8, culminated with an open house in which student work was exhibited through photographs, writings, sculpture, videotaped interviews with students, architectural models, a student-narrated slide show, and a poetry/dance presentation.

Our Renaissance unit is topped off with a performance of a play by William Shakespeare, which, along with the study of Shakespearean theater, constitutes much of the unit itself. In this unit, the culminating event becomes the focal point of the work of the unit.

When they have worked hard and produced exemplary work during a unit of study, the students find it very satisfying to share their results in a celebratory event. While rewarding students for a job well done, we are also promoting positive relations within the school community.

ARTS INTEGRATION

Given time and guidance, I am always amazed at the quality of artistic work that elementary-age students create. The playful quality of art allows students to focus their energies in a way that can be difficult to achieve in any other context. Students respond well to assignments that allow them to learn through their area(s) of strength, and students who shine provide inspiration and motivation for their peers. Cooperative arts projects such as plays, dance performances, puppet shows, architectural models, and murals can also act as a glue that pulls a class together around a unit of study, drawing an image in the mind of each student that lasts for many years.

What is more, art is a subject in which students naturally set personal goals and strive to achieve them, making the arts an ideal vehicle in a multiage setting. In his sixth-grade promotion speech, one student marked his growth over the past several years by noting his increasingly substantial roles in three annual class plays.

For all these reasons, my students and I have always found great satisfaction in projects that integrate the arts within a unit of study.

Arts projects can be framed in numerous ways. My students have written poems about characters in novels and then choreographed movement pieces to accompany readings of their poems. They have written plays about traditional folktales, the history of our town, the individual decades of the twentieth century, the development of the notion of Manifest Destiny in the mid-1800s, and diversity and adversity in twentieth-century America. One year they created a lively and colorful display of geometric designs and optical illusions based on lines, circles, quadrants, symmetry, modular number systems, and flips and rotations. They composed computerized music about twentieth-century issues and outer space, and they sketched detailed line drawings of all parts of a plant and architectural drawings of local historic homes. They manipulated NASA images of the planets on the computer and drew wild sketches of mythological characters and anatomical drawings of imagined adaptations in insects. They sculpted shacks from recycled materials and then wrote about their unseen residents. We visited an art gallery, and they subsequently created movement pieces about the works of art we saw on display.

The arts also have their own integrity as subjects, and we have arts specialists in our building who address these areas, sometimes teaming with us to help carry art concepts into our integrated projects, such as when we consider the work of Renaissance or twentieth-century artists or when we learn about drawing from nature. I take my students' creative work as seriously as I do any assignment, requesting drafts of projects, conferencing with students on possible revisions, and assessing final products through predetermined criteria.

I recently had the opportunity to study and apply an innovative approach to art-based literacy developed by Beth Olshansky of the Laboratory for Interactive Learning at the University of New Hampshire. Using Olshansky's strategies, students first explore a sampling of thematic and powerfully illustrated children's literature, then learn techniques to create their own exemplary works of art, which become the inspiration for their poems and stories. This approach, which has resulted in highly descriptive and figurative writing with students ranging in age from primary grades through high school and with diverse learning styles, is another testament to the power of art-based learning.

When I taught a primary multiage class a number of years ago, we came to a group realization: Art is serious work. It is this attitude that allows creativity to become a legitimate and powerful aspect of the curriculum, fueling student motivation and pride while providing an important vehicle for conceptual and factual understanding and skill development.

RESPONDING TO GROUP LEARNING STYLES

It is crystal clear when an assignment, a topic of study, or an approach to a unit is right for a group of students. They will engage in animated discussions and will come to class speaking about their plans for a work-in-progress. They will ask to skip recess to work on projects and for just ten more minutes at the end of the day to complete their work, or they will even forget completely that the end of the day has arrived. I might even hear a comment or two from parents or community members, or a student might let me know that she is looking forward to carrying out a project she heard about from previous students in the class. Then I know we're on track.

The chemistry and makeup of a particular class is a big factor in determining the level of inspiration and subsequent learning of a group of students, and I have found that it helps to approach each unit guided by the unique identity and qualities of my group. One year our student body was an active group with a strong aptitude for math/science projects, so we immersed ourselves in a rocketry unit involving many challenging design tasks. During the following year, we had a talented group of performers, so we decided to tackle a Shakespearean play. Another year, with a dynamic group of strong-minded individuals, we spent large amounts of time on classroom government.

In this way, I can work within the guidelines of our curriculum while adapting each unit of study to the talents and needs of the class. Because I am familiar with my group of returning students (and I spend some time getting to know incoming students each spring), I have time to think ahead about how best to approach our classroom curriculum.

THE BASICS

We periodically hear concerns about attention to the "basics" in education. Although this notion seems to keep resurfacing, its context has changed through the years. The importance of early literacy skills, for example, has been the focus of much attention and research in recent years. In Vermont, we have been using math and writing portfolios for more than a decade. And as mentioned above, national curriculum standards are pointing to new areas of emphasis in terms of basic skills.

There is a legitimate concern that students need to spend regular amounts of time in the areas of reading, writing, and math and that skill development is an important factor in education. In the multiage classroom, this is not overlooked. One hour is devoted to both math and writing in our classroom every day. We spend thirty minutes each day working directly on reading goals; students are expected to spend the same amount of time reading at home each evening. Twice each week students participate in small group sessions to discuss their readings. Basic skills are presented in an appealing and frequently integrated format, but the goal for students is clear: to become competent readers, writers, and mathematicians. Individual expectations are set according to individual abilities, much as they would be in a single-grade classroom. There are times when this necessitates some ability-level grouping for skill work, but generally accommodations are made in student–teacher conferences.

Skills are subsequently reinforced in all of our other work. Math skills are regularly applied in science and geography and in dealing with social studies data. Reading and writing skills are essential to understanding and responding to written assignments, when conducting research across the curriculum, and particularly when exploring social studies topics. At the intermediate level, students read to learn (as opposed to learning to read). In much the same way, they have begun to apply all their skills in developing an understanding of the world around them.

ACCOMMODATIONS

For most students, skills develop naturally when they are presented clearly and when subsequent assignments reinforce them and provide necessary assessment and feedback. Occasionally, however, a student will need additional support. In these instances, the classroom teacher works closely with the special needs staff.

In our school, as in most Vermont schools, we teach all students in the regular classroom most of the time. Special educators and their aides work with students in the classroom or in small groups in a resource room to help them keep up with the classroom curriculum. When a student is unable to follow along with his or her classmates, accommodations are made, always with a focus on bringing the student to a level of independence by the conclusion of elementary school. Accommodations generally allow students to go along with the unit of study at their own pace and in their own style. This support is particularly important for the younger or weakest special needs students in a multiage classroom.

For instance, in our unit on geology, student groups were asked to prepare a business proposal for a mining company. First, they researched mineral deposits around the world on a computer database to find a suitable location for their mine. Next, they determined the best approach for retrieving the minerals and then reclaiming the land. Students considered the long-range impact of removing a portion of the

Earth's nonrenewable resources. They also found a market for their product and decided how it would best be transported. Finally, each group created and presented an entire business proposal with posters, charts, and graphs. These final proposals were presented to a panel of distinguished guests (the principal and several school board and community members), who assessed the presentations according to a set of predetermined criteria.

This was a challenging project for all students, and special needs students needed quite a bit of support. Working closely with their special education teacher, two of these students together came up with a clear and strong presentation, one that entailed considerably less detail and depth than the others. They focused on just several simplified subtopics and had only one chart each as compared to the numerous cross-referenced charts of the other members of the class. However, because these two students were guided in how to modify the presentation, they presented with confidence and understanding, and no one in the audience considered them less competent than anyone else in the class.

SCHEDULING AND STUDENT CONTRACTS

Learning to use time well is an important objective for intermediate-grade students. For this reason, we include students in the scheduling process. I present my students with a contract each week that states all of their assignments (an example of such a contract is included below). The agreement is that they will complete this work by the end of the week and that they will be given some flexibility in how this comes about. Most of the assignments offer a variety of options to students.

Some parts of the day are inflexible. We have a one-hour math block first thing each morning, when students from several classrooms reshuffle into ability-level math groups. This is followed by an hour-long writer's workshop, a quiet period during which students work on a variety of cross-curricular writing assignments. Special subjects last about forty minutes each day. We hold a fifteen-minute daily class meeting after lunch. The lunch hour includes an indoor and outdoor recess in addition to mealtime. In our case, that leaves us most of each afternoon for everything else.

This large, uninterrupted chunk of time in our schedule is ideal for carrying out in-depth science and social studies projects. When students are given responsibility for a large body of work, it isn't up to the teacher to keep them occupied. After completing an activity or task, they decide what to work on next. This approach creates a more relaxed and less controlled classroom atmosphere.

This student-centered approach requires that students accept responsibility for their learning process. There is a learning curve involved in bringing students to this point, and here is where older students in the class can mentor the younger ones. We discuss ways in which students can pace themselves throughout the week. We post a checklist of work submitted, we have a daily group check-in to help students gauge their progress, and I announce missing work at the end of the week. Students who work efficiently find that they may have time to carry out projects of their own in addition to the assigned work. This is satisfying for both students and teachers.

∘∘

5/6 Contract
February 7–11

Reading: Multicultural America Group Novels

Your three reading goals for Week 1 are due this Wednesday. The three goals include reading, journal entry, and final illustration with quote. On Wednesday, you will begin your goals for Week 2, due next week. Set daily goals for yourself. You will have time most days to work on these goals at school. *You are also expected to work on your goals each night at home until they are completed.*

Language Arts

This week you will complete a first draft of your creative nonfiction essay. In this essay, you become a character who has experienced the issue your group has researched. Share one of your most memorable experiences in the voice of your character. After completing your draft, respond to the self-assessment sheet.

Spelling: Homophones

This week you will be tested on last week's homophones.

Diversity in Twentieth-Century U.S. History

We'll continue to focus on how specific groups of people fared during the past century, exploring the big question:

How have our diverse backgrounds influenced our varied experiences as Americans in the twentieth century?

We will also continue to address this second question in the context of class meetings, cooperative projects, and whole-class lessons. This question asks us to consider the issue of diversity on a personal level:

How can we—each and all—promote e *pluribus unum*?
Abby will work with her research skills group on Tuesday at 1:30 P.M.
I will work with the rest of the class on twentieth-century art forms.
Deborah will not be in this week. We'll see her next week!

HOMEWORK

Monday: *TIME for Kids* and math
Tuesday: reading goals (<u>due tomorrow</u>)
Wednesday: <u>new</u> reading goals and math
Thursday: reading goals, problem solving
Friday: reading goals

ASSESSMENT

In Vermont, we are deeply committed to employing alternative forms of assessment even as we continue to use traditional models. As a multiage teacher who works closely with students over a period of two or three years, I love a quote that I heard at a workshop I attended some years ago: "If the test doesn't agree with what you know about your student, something is wrong with the test."

The advantage we have as multiage teachers is that we come to know our students extremely well. No form of assessment, however valuable, can replace careful and close attentiveness to each individual student and to the dynamics of student groups. At the same time, we clearly need to understand and document what we see in our classrooms. Portfolio assessment and other authentic and performance-based assessment tools allow us to record the details of students' progress with a sharper eye and with a greater sense of meaning, thus helping us hone our skills at student observation. Several examples of assessment tools that I have used in my classroom are reproduced here.

5/6 Problem-Solving Assessment Criteria*

4   Solution is logically supported; it makes mathematical/scientific sense.
    Evidence is completely clear; it's easy to see how you reached your solution.
    Graphics are clear, appropriate, and labeled—charts, graphs, diagrams, etc.
    Math/science vocabulary is used in solution—words, equations, formulas.

3 The solution is logically supported.
A chart may be incompletely labeled or part of evidence may be a bit unclear.
Math/science vocabulary may be weak in places or could be improved.

2 The solution is only partially correct.
Evidence is sketchy or difficult to follow; questions may be raised by a reader.
Graphics are inappropriate or incomplete—labels missing or work unfinished.

1 The solution does not make mathematical/scientific sense; it has serious errors.
Evidence is minimal and incoherent; it's not clear how a solution was reached.

*Holistic scoring guide based on Vermont Math Portfolio criteria.

• •

Theatrical Performance Self-Assessment: Use of Voice

Name:

4 I articulate all of my lines clearly and confidently.
I project all of my lines strongly.
I pause between certain words and sentences to add to the dramatic effect.
I emphasize certain words and lines to add to the dramatic effect.
At times I slow down or speed up to add to the dramatic effect.

3 I articulate most of my lines clearly and confidently.
I project most of my lines strongly.
I pause at times to add to the dramatic effect.
I emphasize certain words or lines to add to the dramatic effect.
I change my pace at least once to add to the dramatic effect.

2 I articulate some of my lines.
I project some of my lines.
I speak slowly enough to be understood.
I use emphasis or change of pace every now and then to add to the effect.

1 I do not articulate or project my lines.
I speak too quickly to be understood.
I do not put any expression into my voice.

Comments on my use of voice:

∘ ∘

Response to Literature Self-Assessment

Name:

Title and Focus

Do I include a fairly short title that relates to the focus?
Does all information in the essay relate to the focus?

Introduction

Do I introduce the book and its author?
Do I introduce each main character in the context of their book?
Do I clearly and concisely (briefly) introduce the focus of my essay?

Body

Does each paragraph begin with a general statement as a topic sentence?
Do I support my general statement with specific examples from my reading?
Do I elaborate on my examples, including analysis?
Do I include at least one quote?
Do I introduce the quote and then discuss its meaning in relation to my focus?
Does all information in each paragraph relate to the topic sentence?

Conclusion

Do I summarize the information in the body of the essay?
Do I wrap up the essay with some reflective comments?

Science Journal Assessment Criteria

5
- responds to question(s)
- explanation uses math/science language as appropriate
- supports information clearly
- clear, labeled diagrams included as needed to support explanations

4
- responds to question(s)
- information is clear and supported but may lack specific or detailed language
- diagrams are clear but may not be completely labeled

3
- responds to question(s)
- information is mostly clear but may not be developed or fully supported
- diagrams missing, minimal, or incomplete (not labeled or finished)

2
- partial response to question(s)
- unclear or unsupported information
- minimal or missing diagrams

1
- does not respond to question(s) in a way that can be understood

REPORTING TO PARENTS

Our multiage classes use the same reporting and conferencing system employed by the rest of our school and school district. We have a trimester program, including three report cards, three midterm progress reports, and two scheduled conferences. The report card combines checklists, narrative information, and optional grades. Along with the report, we include an overview of our classroom curriculum for the marking period. The midterm progress report is a brief narrative to inform parents of their child's overall level of progress.

Beyond these formal methods of communication, there is an enhanced quality in the connection between parents and teachers in multiage classrooms. Contact with the same parents is maintained over several years, thus creating possibilities for more intimate relationships between teachers and families. When a sibling is placed in the same classroom (at the same or different times), this relationship grows even deeper. There is time to develop trust and understanding, leaving parents and teachers more able to work as a team on the child's behalf.

Informal and personal communication occurs more easily when parents and teachers feel comfortable with each other. I encourage parents and students to contact me with their concerns, and I feel free to do the same with them.

TRANSITIONING TO THE NEXT LEVEL

The transition from one multiage classroom to the next one can be challenging for students and parents who have become settled within a particular situation for two or more years, but the shift can be supported in a number of ways. It is important for sending and receiving teachers to be clear about each other's programs so that both can facilitate a smooth transition. Parent communication is valuable at the beginning of the year to help new parents know what to expect and how to assist their child. Through notes and meetings, we discuss our program, teacher expectations, and some of the traits of children at this stage of development. There are also ways to bring a bit of consistency into the multiage program across grade levels. This can be done through careful sequencing of the curriculum and expectations from one classroom to the next, through teaming of classes across grade levels, and through whole-school units or events.

We hold a transition day each spring, when students spend a morning in their future classroom. This offers a wonderful opportunity for students and teachers to start to get to know each other in preparation for the coming school year. Students transitioning to middle school also have a transition program in which they spend an afternoon visiting their new classrooms and teachers.

3

SOCIAL DEVELOPMENT IN THE INTERMEDIATE MULTIAGE CLASSROOM

As the members of our class sit perched on their desks for our first meeting of the school year, returning students display an almost exaggerated nonchalance. We begin with words of welcome and encouragement to our new students.

"Don't worry," Audrey, a fifth grader, offers. "I remember feeling so nervous on my first day of school last year. But other kids helped me whenever I was confused, and pretty soon I got comfortable."

If I had to name the single greatest advantage of multiage classrooms, it would be the benefit to which Audrey alluded. Every member of the classroom community shares the work of transmitting the classroom culture from one year to the next. In this way, a multiage program constantly builds on itself.

CLASSROOM CULTURE

"Did you remember to order *TIME for Kids* again this year?" Josie asks me in September, reminding me of my pledge to her last June. "I still have all my issues from last year."

When I answer this question affirmatively, she runs off to share the good news with her classmates. Her positive attitude about current events has already begun to impact the group, and new students are anxious to receive their first copy of this student periodical. Episodes such as this one illustrate how carryover from year to year impacts every aspect of social and academic life in the classroom.

Some years ago, the students in our class decided to organize a spring party as an after-school fund-raiser. They appointed groups of students to record dance tapes, organize refreshments, coordinate games, and recruit parent chaperones. The event was quite a success, and it even raised a bit of money. For years afterward, students would look toward this event each year with great anticipation, and returning students were quick to take charge. The annual party, evolving along with the dynamics of each group, became a thread in the fabric of our program. Recently, students initiated a new fund-raising tradition: a school store on wheels.

Technological skills are also passed along by returning students. Each year, as in all classrooms, several students rise to the surface as technological experts. The benefit of our multiage setting is that returning experts begin the school year familiar with the kinds of technology available in our classroom, and they are enthusiastically prepared to share their skills. A high level of technological awareness has become part of the identity of our grades 5/6 multiage program.

When students assume more responsibility for initiating new students, the teacher has more opportunity to reflect on the current program and generate innovations. In the case of technology education, for example, the easy transmission of current tech skills allows me to keep pace with emerging technologies. I am thus able to add new computer skills and software to our repertoire each year.

What happens, in effect, is that the fluid transmission of a classroom culture paves the way for its evolution as well. And because teachers are less caught up in setting standards and expectations each year, they are also freer to observe and consider the nature of a particular group of students and to create possibilities for the optimal development of each learner.

As in any classroom, ours has a distinct and recognizable tone and character each year. The multiage teacher, working with a more independent group from the outset, can nurture a deeper awareness of individual students and is also more able to respond to the needs of the group. Individual assignments, as well as entire units of study, can be adapted to make them meaningful and challenging for all students. The multiage configuration allows me to come to know the students in our room to an extent that enables me to guide them as individuals.

STRUCTURED SOCIALIZING AND COOPERATIVE LEARNING

Two students approach me with their story drafts and peer assessment sheets. "We're going out in the hallway to conference," they inform me. Fifteen minutes later, I notice one of the students using feedback he received to further revise his story. He explains that his partner offered a good idea for developing the details in his piece. Meanwhile, his partner is fine-tuning her paragraph structure.

This vignette offers an example of the *structured socializing* and *cooperative learning* that are central elements in our intermediate multiage classroom. Since incoming students are introduced to peer conferencing by returning students, we are able to begin this sort of collaboration early in the school year. To establish a responsible approach to structured socializing, I start the year with small groups of two students and clearly defined roles. As students' social skills develop, we gradually include the use of larger groups as well. I also request that groups be multiage (and sometimes also mixed gender), though I often allow students to choose partners. This satisfies students' desire for autonomy while assuring they will mix across ages right from the start.

One early project for partners was a mini-research presentation on a subtopic related to our current thematic unit on communication in colonial America. Each pair was asked to research and interpret an early American political cartoon that I had provided, to present their conclusions to the class, and to hang their written explanations beside the cartoons on a wall chart. This project involved reading, discussion, collaborative problem solving, writing, and public speaking. Expectations were specified for each step along the way.

As the year moves along, students get more in the swing of cooperative group work. They are soon able to benefit from opportunities for creative collaboration in response to a more broadly defined task. In the case of the sample project just outlined, this burgeoning collaboration was evidenced by October of that school year, when groups of four to five students were invited to create a movement/theater piece depicting a particular conflict or challenge from colonial times. I asked that the groups be both multiage and mixed gender. Topics addressed included:

- lack of understanding between colonists and Native Americans;
- quest for the Northwest Passage funded by wealthy businessmen;

- intolerance of Puritans toward change within their community;
- issues arising between colonists and the British king and Parliament.

The students' dance pieces grew and developed over a period of weeks, as I gave the groups a new direction for elaborating their piece each week, as follows:

- Form a series of body sculptures to represent your issue.
- Find interesting and appropriate ways to move between sculptures.
- Research and compose a written introduction to the piece.
- Add suitable period music and adjust your movements accordingly.

(The order in which these tasks were assigned could, of course, be rearranged for a different emphasis.)

In the early part of this process, our main focus was on negotiating through challenges within the interpersonal dynamics of each group. I walked from group to group, acting as a facilitator. In one group, a student felt that other members were not hearing his suggestions; we negotiated a way for the group to take his views more seriously. In another group, the girls felt that the boys were uncooperative; the boys were encouraged to offer more verbal input to the group. One particular student had difficulty taking the project seriously, but as he experienced his ability to contribute to an effective performance, his focus within the group improved. One student was reluctant to participate at all; he was provided with a technical support role, though he subsequently asked to rejoin his group. Eventually, each group evolved an active and engaged collaboration among all of its members.

Works-in-progress were presented to the whole class for feedback at the end of each session. Effective aspects were noted, along with constructive suggestions. Feedback focused on the latest aspect of the piece. Peer critique was invaluable, but frequently the most beneficial aspects were the experiences of performing the piece in front of an audience of peers and of observing the possibilities presented in the work of other groups. After these presentations, each group engaged in lively discussion about potential further refinement of their own work.

Eventually, we performed our compositions at a school assembly. This culmination was satisfying and important, though the actual process of collaboration was where most social growth occurred. Performance pieces provide an excellent laboratory for students' development of co-operative skills, because each person's individual contribution clearly affects the whole work.

Returning students were an asset in the entire process. Their previous experiences in working on creative projects applied to challenging academic material allowed them to act as models and leaders in their respective groups. Thus the project was more truly child-centered, and I was freed to serve as the guide and helper.

UNSTRUCTURED SOCIALIZING

Our school sits beneath Mount Abraham and a series of smaller foothills. The New Haven River, cascading down from the mountain, passes alongside our school, marking the boundary of our recess field. When spring ice breaks up in the mountains and forces its way downstream, it sounds like a train roaring by, and my students rush to the window to view the river at its wildest.

At recess, I stand on the edge of this magnificent schoolyard and glance around. In the distance, a group of high-energy students is immersed in a game of football. As more students spill out of the building, some filter in with this group. Across the field, a smaller group of students is perfecting its snow sculpture collection—a high-backed chair, a long low couch, and a big television screen, which they are fancifully detailing. Between the two ends of the playground, students run across an elaborate wooden play structure designed and built by parents several years ago. Meanwhile, pairs and trios of more reflective individuals amble around the field in quiet conversation.

This scene repeats itself with occasional and seasonal variations throughout the school year, as students develop a network of social relationships. Students freely form themselves into groups across age, ability, gender, and personality types. I attribute this openness both to our small supportive community and to our multiage approach. The students in our school know and accept one another.

Unstructured socializing occurs inside the classroom as well. In addition to outdoor recess breaks, we have a daily "explore time"—twenty minutes during which students are free to engage in any activity of their choice in the classroom. Popular explore time activities include sketching, painting, using the computer, listening to music, playing the synthesizer keyboard, and talking to friends. Students also use this time to catch up on classwork, though by student and parent request, only one break each day is generally used for this purpose.

One of the most common concerns of parents new to the intermediate multiage program is that fourth and fifth graders are exposed socially to sixth graders. Early in the school year, we may, in fact, hear about rough language on the playground from the parent of a younger student. These issues tend to fade quickly, as each student finds a comfortable social niche. Parents who have experienced multiage settings in the primary grades understand that there is an adjustment period when a child enters a new class, and they also anticipate the long-range benefits once their child has made this adjustment.

Sometimes a new intermediate student will become quite infatuated with a group of older students. This situation most frequently occurs with a student who is the oldest child in his or her family. The multiage program offers this child an opportunity to experience being the younger child for a change. This may create a short-term challenge during the subsequent year, when all the child's friends have moved on; however, the student generally finds renewed friendships with his or her peers after a period of grieving the loss of previous years' bonds.

CLASS MEETINGS

Years ago in one of my graduate classes in education, a wise presenter advised us that "a pressing social issue in the classroom is best dealt with immediately. It is worth putting all else aside to resolve a concern that is already distracting students from their academic tasks at hand." I took this advice to heart in my early years of teaching, when I worked with primary students in a small private school. Neither the administration nor the parents were attached to the idea of covering a preset body of academic material, so I felt free to balance traditional academics with social and creative time. Once, on an afternoon when I was immersed in paperwork alongside my students, Caitlin approached me.

"Our class library is a mess again. We need to have a meeting," the seven-year-old informed me.

"Why don't you and Claire run the meeting today?" I suggested to her, distracted with my own project; so off they went.

Observing my students facilitate this meeting was a powerful experience for me. The two girls modeled my leadership style, right down to using my verbal expressions. "We're not blaming anyone for this problem," they parroted. "We forget to put our books away sometimes, too. But we need some suggestions." Never again did I doubt my impact as a teacher. I also came to respect the ability of young people to settle their own affairs, given an appropriate forum and structure.

After working with upper-elementary students in a public school for several years, I became increasingly aware of academic pressures. Administration seemed focused on raising student achievement scores and addressing an expansive curriculum. Vocal parents wanted assurance that we were not padding the curriculum with too much fluff. My class sizes were increasing, and along with that, I was challenged by the behavior issues more typical of older students. I felt less comfortable spending time hanging out with my students and talking about what was on their minds, especially among my classroom full of preadolescents, who had some difficulty hearing one another out.

Yet as I began combing through the literature on discipline strategies, I realized, just as my presenter suggested years ago, that holding class meetings and improving listening skills were exactly what we needed to be doing more of. Drawing on some elements of William Glasser's model, I initiated daily class meetings, and soon our entire school followed suit. It took several weeks to establish our meeting guidelines and structure, but then we were off and running.

Daily meetings, lasting fifteen minutes, begin with appreciations offered optionally by each person in attendance. We spend time each year discussing the nature of a sincere appreciation; this portion of the meeting creates a positive tone in which to discuss more difficult issues. (Even on the occasional days when we don't have time for a full meeting, students request time for appreciations.) We move from appreciations to old business and finally to new agenda items.

The students create our meeting agenda in a posted list. Meeting topics are noted alongside the student's name and the date. We address items in their order of occurrence, unless there is an item of immediate concern. Initially, the agenda was created entirely by students. That first year, our students needed to know that class meetings were truly their own forum. Now adults in the room also submit items occasionally.

Intermediate students are likely to raise different issues than those presented by students in the primary grades. Whereas my primary students generally brought up playground issues and concerns about the behavior of their peers, my intermediate students rarely broach such issues in class. (In fact, it is frequently parents who inform me about issues that have arisen at school among the students with whom I work daily.) The issues raised by my older students generally address their personal rights and responsibilities in the school community: the right to wear hats indoors; suggested adjustments to classroom or school behavior plans; the coordination of social events, fund-raisers, and field trips. True to their developmental stage, my intermediate students look for ways to empower and validate themselves as a group.

It is also interesting to observe the changing dynamics between older and younger students in the classroom during meetings. At first, most younger students are predictably more reluctant to speak out on controversial issues until they get a feel for the views of their older classmates. As the year progresses, this dynamic changes, and most students come to express their views freely. This results in more interesting and animated discussions among the members of the class.

I have had only marginal success in allowing my intermediate students to run their own meetings, though each year we give it a try. Perhaps the problem is my discomfort with the chaos that ensues when a sizable group of preteens gathers to discuss a somewhat controversial issue without clearly enforced guidelines. Whatever the case, a teacher generally facilitates our intermediate class meetings, although students do most of the talking. This maintains student empowerment while allowing for efficient meetings that are thus able to address the students' own concerns. (Students repeatedly request that we limit meetings to a fifteen-minute time frame.) Occasionally, when a particularly delicate issue arises, a student facilitator is appointed, and the adult(s) leave the room for a period of time to allow the group to work things out on its own. When a strong and impartial leader is chosen, this can work well.

At one of the first class meetings each school year, students create a list of classroom expectations in terms of behavior. Although teachers may need to help enforce these guidelines, the guidelines themselves remain posted and intact for the school year.

While the class meeting is not the panacea for every social ill that arises at school, it certainly creates a positive tone of shared responsibility and student validation. In this sense, it is an essential component of a student-centered multiage classroom.

DISCIPLINE STRATEGIES

At some point in the year, a handful of our sixth graders can become restless and defiant, as they enter adolescence and prepare internally for their transition to seventh grade. This impacts the tone in our classroom. My colleagues and I notice that this phenomenon, often a significant problem in single sixth-grade classes, gets diluted in multiage classrooms. In the 4/5/6 classroom, the eruption can be almost insignificant, depending upon the nature of the group. In a 5/6 combination, one or two fifth graders may decide to follow suit with their sixth-grade peers.

The activities we engage in require that students take responsibility for a high level of self-monitoring. If this becomes difficult for them and the situation threatens to get out of hand, we move to a more structured discipline system, again drawing on elements from Glasser's model. This system is directly based on the guidelines established by students at the beginning of the year, though sometimes it is more specific. For example, one of the student-written guidelines several years ago stated, "Respect each student's right to learn in the classroom." After some difficulty with attentiveness during group discussions, we specified, "Give attention to the person who is speaking." (In response, students were more specific in developing their own guidelines the subsequent year.) We limit our revised guidelines to five or six essential behaviors. We present our list to students and ask if there are any objections to these expectations. There may be some discussion of wording, but there are generally no substantial objections to the expected behaviors. In fact, most or all students admit that the lack of observance of these behaviors has been getting in our way.

At this point, we establish a sequence of consequences for disregarding the expectations. We explain that since some students have been unable to monitor themselves, we feel the need to assist them. This is the least-popular aspect of our plan and the one in which we initially offer less room for negotiation; but since the students have agreed that there is a need for setting limits, they are willing to go along with it. The sequence of increasingly serious consequences generally involves a verbal reminder, a plan written by the student and signed by the teacher and a parent, a consequence or community service specified in the student's plan, and a meeting between the parent, teacher, and principal. There is also another option, available at any point. A student who is feeling restless may request or be asked to work in another self-chosen area of the building for a period of time. This location is usually a primary classroom or the school library.

This system tends to reestablish a learning atmosphere in the classroom with little fanfare, as students begin to internalize appropriate behaviors. Most students who have difficulty with appropriate behavior never get beyond the written plan, as this is the point when they generally decide to self-monitor. As our classroom tone improves, there is less need for such tight control and students may begin to renegotiate aspects of our plan, thus placing responsibility for behavior back where it belongs—with the students.

ADAPTATIONS FOR INDIVIDUAL STUDENTS

Occasionally, there are students with issues such as ADHD (attention-deficit hyperactivity disorder) who need a more personally tailored behavior plan. We generally encourage them to attempt to follow the established guidelines, as these students tend to benefit from clear structures. However, a student or his/her parents may suggest slight modifications to the consequences. For instance, some students are offered the option of short time-outs in the hallway during which they are encouraged to get themselves more centered.

I have also been inspired by child psychologist Robert Brooks's observation that disconnected students benefit greatly from special responsibilities at school. These roles give students a sense of ownership and belonging that results in more positive behaviors and attitudes. For example, one rather restless child who loved gadgets became our audiovisual monitor. Whenever a VCR or overhead projector was needed in our room, he took responsibility for signing it out, picking it up, getting it set up, and returning it. This responsibility also involved choosing a student helper, thus offering further empowerment. Another active student, a technologically oriented individual, became our computer monitor, which involved checking our computers and software each day for proper use, rebuilding the computer desktops each month, and being on hand to assist students as the need arose. A third easily distracted student, one who always offered to help out, became the classroom job monitor. Whenever students were absent, he saw to their classroom chores. Their special roles empowered these students and gave them something productive to do with their restless energy.

STUDENT–TEACHER RELATIONSHIPS

"Can I speak to you in private for a moment?" a sixth grader requests on one of the last days of the school year, so we step into a side room as other students shuffle out to recess. "I want to apologize for all the hard times I've given you over the past two years," this bright and sometimes feisty sixth grader confides. "You may think this sounds silly, and please don't tell anyone I've said so, but you're a great teacher and I've really come to love you."

As young people move toward adolescence, their relationship with the adults in their lives begins to shift. Students begin to question and at times challenge the views and approaches of persons in authority. They begin to act out social postures in front of their peers, and these stances can place them in ungraceful situations. Conflicting emotions can become stressful, confusing, and overwhelming for even the most centered students.

The best way I have found to work with this normal phase of development is to create clear and consistent classroom guidelines while forming a supportive personal relationship with each individual student, a relationship that encourages open and respectful dialogue. I can picture numerous challenging situations among the students with whom I have worked, yet I cannot recall a single student with whom I have not developed a close and caring relationship over the span of two to three years. Frequently, this relationship blossoms in the second or even third year.

A former colleague of mine, a Montessori teacher-educator who worked in a multiage elementary setting, was fond of saying, "Parents have a somewhat irrational relationship with their children, and single-grade teachers generally have a rational relationship with their students. In our case, after working with a child for several years, we also have a somewhat irrational relationship with our students." This was a humorous way of saying, as my student pointed out above, that a deep bond grows between a teacher and a student who have been through shared experiences over the course of two or three years. This relationship is one in which teacher and child come to know each other very well, form an intuitive understanding, and become a part of each other's lives, at least for a period of time.

Students occasionally come back to me several years after moving on to high school, requesting a letter of reference for entrance into a special program. "You are the teacher who has known me the best," is how one boy put it. Likewise, I take deep pleasure in watching my students mature after leaving our classroom, as they move through high school and beyond. Frequently, I will teach their siblings after them, sometimes working with a particular family for six or seven years. (This year I have a student in class who was born the year her older sister was in my class *twelve years ago,* my first year at the Lincoln Community School.) When I run into former students or their parents, we stop and chat, and it feels like meeting up with part of my big extended family.

Truly, the student–teacher relationship is at the heart of education, and my approach to this relationship is woven into all the anecdotes I offer in this book. Like the parent–child relationship, it is composed of a balancing act between moving in and standing back, providing support structures and offering freedom, acting as both teacher and learner, guide and guided, observer and observed.

STUDENT–STUDENT INTERACTIONS AND RELATIONSHIPS

For a number of years, my intermediate students would start the day each Tuesday morning by walking down to the kindergarten room and reading with their KINtime (Kindergarten-Intermediate Time) partners for twenty minutes. During this stretch of time, some forty students were spread about the room, half of them reading aloud with great animation while their younger partners listened with enraptured attention. Every adult present could have left the room unnoticed. This behavior was consistent even among some students who were otherwise quite easily distracted. Once, after one of these sessions, I asked my class, "How is it that you are so completely attentive with your KINtime partners, even on days when you have such a difficult time staying focused on your own assignments?"

Ole replied, "They think we're the best thing in the whole world, so we just can't let them down."

Being seen as knowledgeable and competent is hugely important to all of us, and studies repeatedly show that students rise to the level that is expected of them. In a multiage setting, older students are admired by the younger ones, and this experience paves the way for many individuals to shine as competent leaders. Just as important and productive is the way in which older students in a multiage classroom serve as role models to younger ones. Younger students are provided with older peers who have been where they are going and can help guide the way. One year several sixth-grade girls established a student newspaper. A short while later, two fifth-grade girls decided to start a school food shelf, commenting that they wanted to take on a project of their own, just as the older girls had done. Neither of these activities had ever been done independently before by students in our class, and it was clear that the older girls inspired the younger ones to take on a significant initiative of their own.

As the year progresses, new student friendships form across age levels. When I continue to ask students to form cooperative groups across grade levels, it becomes increasingly apparent that bonds are forming. This is also obvious on the playground and during indoor explore time. There is a bright excitement in the eyes of a younger student who is taken under the wing of an older one. And as noted above, the older student stands a little taller and prouder when given this enthusiastic acknowledgment.

Shifting social dynamics can also be a cause of stress among intermediate students. While there is growth in the process of learning to get along with a variety of people, there are also times when old friends are left out and feelings are hurt. Sometimes a student returns from recess with teary eyes, requesting the opportunity to meet with a friend in the hallway to "work things out." I've found it's important to offer intermediate students the opportunity to work out friendship issues on their own. Preadolescents have a strong sense of privacy and feel quite uncomfortable when it is invaded, even though they continue to need lots of support and some guidance in developing social skills.

Our school counselor does a wonderful job of creating multiage student friendship groups in which my students explore their unfolding social lives in a supportive and nurturing setting. On occasion, the counselor also works with our whole class to address a particular issue. It can be satisfying and revealing at these times to switch from classroom facilitator to unobtrusive group member and to see my students in another light.

The most dramatic change we see as students progress from primary to intermediate grades is a shifting loyalty from adults to peers. The challenge for me as a teacher is to respect and support this changing allegiance while offering a steady relationship to my students, even though I know it is unlikely that I will receive a consistent response back from them. And yet, as my students occasionally remind me, we adults are far more significant to them than they let on.

CELEBRATIONS AND RITUALS

In our community, there is a small social hall where our sixth graders are officially promoted to the seventh grade each spring in a social event of increasingly significant proportion. The event begins weeks before the actual ceremony. Sometime in May, sixth graders and their classroom teachers spend a day at the Pine Ridge Ropes Course, engaged in challenge-by-choice and trust-building activities designed to prepare students for the social challenges of middle school.

Back at school that day, the younger students in our two classrooms each choose a sixth grader to honor with a skit, card, medal, work of art, speech, gift, or some combination thereof. These presentations are worked on secretively for a couple of weeks and are presented in an informal gathering at school just before the sixth graders head off to the hall to rehearse their processional.

This is a joyful and sad gathering. After all of the presentations, students and teachers spontaneously come up to share their thoughts and feelings. It's a time for sixth graders to speak from the heart about their experiences with their classmates over the years and about the bonds that have been made across age groups and are about to be severed, at least for a year or two. Laughter and tears highlight this event.

After lunch, Bill Roleau, a Lincoln resident who assists us annually, arrives at school with his horse and wagon piled with hay bales to carry the sixth-grade class to the hall for rehearsal, just a mile from our school. Younger classmates wave them off, and they disappear slowly down the road. A few parents are generally on hand to capture the moment on film.

As soon as the rehearsal is over, parents hustle in to add final decorative touches to the hall, adorning it with flowers, streamers, and balloons. A central stairway to the stage is temporarily installed so that students can march down the center aisle and directly up to the stage. A large embellished archway is placed at the beginning of this aisle, forming another perfect photo opportunity. Two fifth graders from each classroom have been chosen by sixth graders to act as ushers and hand out the program as guests arrive. This task is considered a huge honor, and ushers are expected to dress in formal attire.

My task is to keep the ceremony within a one-hour time limit. The procession is accompanied by live music, provided by varying staff, students, and community members. The principal and teachers offer words of inspiration. A handful of sixth graders write and present speeches, and these can be a highlight of the event. As students are presented with their diplomas, teachers share personal anecdotes that portray some aspects of each student's individuality. After two or three years, we have plenty to choose from. We end the ceremony with a slide show that includes photos of the graduates growing from birth through sixth grade. Finally, students march out as proud seventh graders, into a receiving line and a social gathering at which they are the stars. As entertainment for the reception, the sixth-grade group often prepares a comic routine in which they reflect upon their years in elementary school.

While this event focuses on sixth graders, it is truly a multiage occasion. As younger students watch their older classmates prepare to move on, they are themselves preparing to assume the role of older students and eventually to face the experience of leaving elementary school behind them. In previous years, the sixth graders created symbolic wills for their younger classmates, leaving behind parts of themselves to specific students. Our annual tradition is enhanced by the emotional factor of younger students witnessing this rite of passage for their older classmates. Each year parents and community members remark on the power of this celebration that marks the end of elementary school and the beginning of a new phase of life. It helps all of us accept and learn from the changes in these emerging members of our community.

We share many other school traditions: camping trips, field trips, and assorted classroom celebrations. Each event is meaningful for our students and builds on our shared experiences, yet none seems quite as poignant as the events surrounding sixth-grade promotion.

SOCIAL BENEFITS AND CONCERNS

During my twenty years as a primary and intermediate multiage teacher, I have noticed that certain conditions result in optimal benefits in my classroom. Because situations are often less than the ideal, it's worthwhile to be aware of potential challenges.

In a true multiage classroom, at least half the students return each year. If this is not the case, the benefit of carryover from one year to the next is lost. There are not enough students to assimilate the new ones, and the teacher must once again assume primary responsibility for integrating a large group of students. The teacher will likewise spend much energy getting to know a large group of children each year, losing the benefits of continuity from year to year.

The chemistry in a classroom is an essential factor in its success. When placing students in a multiage classroom, it's important to realize that students at each age level will likely be together for several years.

For this reason, selecting a compatible mix of individuals is important. When dynamics are quite discordant, we occasionally switch students between intermediate classrooms before they have completed the full multiage cycle. Similarly, a parent or teacher may feel that a particular child would be better off in a different classroom setting, and this judgment is weighed carefully. If the majority of the group remains intact, multiage benefits are not lost, and the individuals concerned will be in situations where they can achieve greater success.

Students can benefit most from the multiage experience in a student-centered classroom in which they are asked to assume responsibility for many aspects of their learning experience and where a teacher is able to respond to their needs. This requires teachers, administrators, and parents who are comfortable with a flexible approach that offers students many choices and considerable freedom. It requires a curriculum that can be adapted to the needs of a mixed-age group.

In traditional classrooms of the past, it was assumed that older students need less space to move around in than younger students do. To this day, classrooms for intermediate students tend to be smaller than those for primary students. We now know how important it is for people of all ages to move around, and this could not be more true in an intermediate multiage classroom that fosters independence—and interdependence—in students. One of the best ways I have seen to prevent classroom conflicts is to provide students with plenty of space. When this is not possible in the classroom, I seek ways to provide space options in other parts of the building. Frequently, this is all a restless student needs to get calmed down.

CLASSROOM LAYOUT AND SUPPLIES IN A MULTIAGE CLASSROOM

Inviting student input into the use of classroom space promotes a sense of responsibility in the multiage classroom. Several returning students generally help me unpack and shelve new materials and arrange furniture the week before school starts. At the beginning of the year, I often pair a returning student with a new student and request that they work at a shared desk. Once the younger students are transitioned in, all students are free to work where they please. However, during presentations and silent work periods, I generally ask students to remain at their home-base seats. The students and I decide upon these together, so the seating plan works well from both of our perspectives. Students enjoy rearranging our desks every couple of months. We also regroup desks according to the needs of our current unit. Our Shakespeare units, for instance, require a setup that allows desks to be cleared and stacked to provide a rehearsal space. A previous chemistry unit called for students to work with partners, while a former art-based project involved groups of four sharing a set of materials.

Classroom supplies are accessed in several areas. Students keep their personal books, notebooks, and journals in individual cubbies in our coat area. We also use movable storage boxes that can be tucked under desks so students don't have to constantly go back and forth to their cubbies. Classroom books, manipulatives, papers, and most art materials are stored on open shelves around the classroom. Scissors, pencils, pencil sharpeners, markers, and colored pencils are kept in small shared art supply boxes on student desks. I've found that things work most smoothly when materials used most frequently are readily available to students. This, of course, must be balanced with the need for open desk space.

CONFIDENCE, CREATIVITY, AND FREEDOM

A wonderful benefit of multiage classrooms is that each student finds a niche and an identity for several years, a place where she or he is known and an identity that is understood and accepted. This creates a feeling of confidence that allows students to express their creativity and take risks.

In my mind, I still clearly see two former students—a lofty sixth grader and a tiny fourth grader—offering a short presentation to our class some years ago. The older girl towers over her partner, yet the younger child is the more competent student. As they look up and down at each other, they stand confidently in front of our class, jointly offering the results of their investigation in clear voices, two girls so completely different that it is simultaneously touching and humorous. We can all work together, they show me as I review this scene in my mind. That's what's so great about the multiage classroom.

4

MULTIAGE LANGUAGE ARTS

Leaf Map

I have a land,
and like all lands it has a map.
You and others may call it
                    different.
            Why?
        Why, might I ask?
        A leaf,
        a maple leaf,
        you
            and
            only you call it.
Its cascading misty-like gold
indicates that it is always day,
but the calm healing-like red
    tells that it is always dawn.
The veins indicate high ridges
The three main and highest
            are
uninhabited and too high for trees.
        Bug bites
            in my leaf
        tell of seas,

lakes,
ponds,
water bodies—
unusual ones,
ones with treasures,
treasures unknown,
ones with waves
that are
murderous,
ones that have islands
so small,
tiny,
that only one tree
grows on them.
Smaller and lighter
veins
wander about, making
shapes like you
have never imagined.
But all these shapes
are the sites of
the many towns
and villages.
My map is not normal,
but then again,
who would want
to be normal?

—Ruth Bernstein

This poem, written by one of my intermediate students several years ago, says much about the value of an integrated curriculum that allows students to make connections across topics and subjects. Language is a thread that helps us weave together and express the many aspects of education and life that often seem so fragmented. As learners in the world, we all try to make sense of our lives and those around us. In a rich language arts program, we can reach for this highest goal. In the process of gathering and sharing information and stories, discussing and debating ideas, interpreting perceptions, and expressing understandings and beliefs, students articulate a sense of identity and wholeness. In the multiage classroom, the poetry of one insightful student can inspire classmates and help them develop a deeper understanding of metaphor.

OVERALL PLAN

Formally, our language arts program is divided into the four traditional areas of reading, writing, listening, and speaking. In daily classroom life, these areas merge with one another and integrate with the entire curriculum. To clarify the roles of each of these categories, however, it will be useful to take a look at each one individually.

Reading

Reading occurs in many formats throughout the day, both formally and informally. Our formal program consists of group-read novels and shorter readings selected for their developmental appropriateness, literary value, and connection to a current unit of study. Students independently complete weekly reading assignments paired with a weekly essay question that is later discussed in a small group. Students often take ownership for their weekly literature groups through a series of rotating role assignments. These roles may include discussion director, vocabulary enricher, illustrator, connector, acting director, and investigator. At the end of a group-read novel, each student writes a reflective essay in response to one of several possible questions designed to link the book with a central concept of study.

Generally, I look for a group of novels that develops a subtheme from our unit of study. During our unit on homes and architecture, we read about homelessness. For our space unit, we read science fiction. For our unit on the Renaissance, we read novels that showed the influence of travel on that time period. Each of these readings also led to interesting writing assignments: poems about homelessness, original science fiction tales, and short stories in which characters and plot were developed in a Renaissance setting.

I also like to pull packets of fiction and nonfiction readings together to assure a common body of knowledge on a particular topic. For example, in our study of Greek mythology, I prepared a series of readings and follow-up activities about the culture of ancient Greece. In American studies, we read short historic tales about events from each time period. During our unit on Shakespeare, students read about the Elizabethan Renaissance. These sorts of assignments help reinforce the students' skills in reading for information while expanding their content knowledge.

Students have opportunities to choose their own readings, though I may define categories of readings such as biographical novels, Newbery

Medal winners, or American literature. When reading within one of these categories, I assign focused freewrites and book talks or final projects that can be shared with the class. After completing a marathon of reading selections, we sometimes enjoy a book celebration, where we share our projects along with some edible treats.

The other group reading we engage in regularly involves current events. While I have used a variety of formats, I find that students enjoy the weekly news periodicals published for students. These come with informative teacher's guides and interesting activities for students. I look for one that is designed for a range of grades, or else I choose a reading level that is in the middle range of my students. Because we spend the majority of class time focusing on big unit topics that may have little connection with the present, news periodicals help assure that my students are informed about important current issues and events. Frequently, the articles spark informal discussions among students, and many of them collect and save these periodicals for their entire time in our classroom.

We do not use textbooks in our classroom for the content areas. Instead, we gather a collection of books about our current topic of study, and these become student reference books throughout the unit. These resources are supplemented by CD-ROM reference materials and the Internet. I encourage and monitor topic-based reading with focused assignments. For instance, my students were asked to write a series of poems about characters from Greek mythology, including at least three significant facts about each character. Within minutes, students were pouring through our classroom book collection and taking notes for their poems.

Finally, I spend a portion of each day reading aloud to my students. They love this time, even though they are all fluent readers. I generally read novels or stories related to our current unit of study, thus building our shared literary knowledge and strengthening our classroom culture. We sometimes have the opportunity to reflect on characters or themes across our readings. In our recent class reading of *The Tempest,* for example, the students immediately saw a parallel between the relationship between Prospero and Ariel and that of Oberon and Puck from *A Midsummer Night's Dream,* the play we had studied and performed earlier in the year.

Writing

Writing occurs throughout the day but with greatest focus during our hour-long writer's workshop each morning. Students compose prose and poetry in response to formal assignments, they record ideas and solutions to math and science problems and investigations, they gather informational notes on research topics in social studies, they freewrite in their journals, and they jot down notes to their friends. More than any other skill, writing permeates the entire curriculum as a means by which students can demonstrate understanding. Because of the broad range of abilities in a multiage classroom, there is a need to adjust expectations to the needs of individuals, even when the initial assignment is consistent for the entire group. This personalization unfolds naturally from the teacher's understanding of individual students' needs and capabilities.

We use a writing process approach. Students generally have one formal writing assignment that they carry out over the course of one or more weeks. Assignments alternate, including such genres as creative and personal narratives, reflective and critical essays, research reports, responses to literature, formal correspondence, and poetry. (Content-related writing is also discussed in subsequent chapters.) Students complete a draft, then conference with the teacher, a peer, or both before beginning on a final draft.

The Vermont Writing Portfolio forms a basis for discussing the writing genres mentioned above, excluding poetry. We read and discuss benchmark pieces in each of these categories, and students strive to compose writing that meets or exceeds the standards exemplified by these pieces. We consider the five Vermont Writing Portfolio criteria across all genres: purpose, organization, details, voice and tone, and writing conventions (see sample essay guidelines below). Students are introduced to the genres and criteria one by one through writing exercises designed to draw on their strengths. This process is facilitated by the fact that half the class is already familiar with the writing portfolio program and student conferencing methods. With a student's permission, we sometimes conference as a class on a particular piece of writing, noting effective passages and overall strengths and suggesting possible revisions. This serves as a model for peer conferencing.

◦◦◦

Revising an Essay

When you revise a paper, remember that revision is something much different than editing for surface errors. Consider these portfolio criteria:

Purpose   Do you have <u>one</u> clear focus in your piece, or do you hop from event to event?

Do you include a topic sentence to emphasize the subtopic of each paragraph?
Does each subtopic relate to the overall focus?
Make sure you end up with a strong central focus or theme.

Organization   Does your piece have a beginning, middle, and end?
Does each paragraph lead into the next one to move the piece along?
Have you placed everything in its place in your piece for a good reason?

Details   Do you create an experience for your reader, or do you just list events?
Be sure to use specific nouns, strong verbs, and descriptive language.
Can your reader sense the people, things, and situations you describe?
Have you included all senses: sight, sound, touch, taste, and smell?

Voice and Tone   Do you <u>show</u> (not tell) your personality and feelings to your reader?
Does your writing create a mood or perspective for the reader?
Do you vary your sentence structure and sentence length?

Once your revise your paper, you can begin editing. This includes checking for grammar, usage, and mechanics (G.U.M.). For more specifics, use the "Editing Checklist." Here's an overview:

G.U.M.   Have you written in full sentences?
Have you used capitals, periods, quotes, and other punctuation correctly?
Have you corrected your spelling?
Have you remembered paragraph breaks?
Have you used words correctly, including homophones such as "their" and "too"?
Have you made sure that your grammar is correct?

PLEASE KEEP THIS GUIDE IN YOUR WRITING SECTION FOR FUTURE USE.

These guidelines are useful when conferencing on a draft.

✻✻

When I taught a primary class, we published a monthly class magazine in which each student submitted her or his best piece of writing for that time period. In this way, parents were able to observe their own child's progress in the context of a larger group of student writing. Parents would frequently comment on the progress of other children in the class besides their own, and students used the magazine as a standard by which they evaluated their own work. I remember one student reflecting on her work: "This isn't good enough for the magazine," she decided, returning to her desk to bring it up to a higher standard.

Now, working with intermediate students, we publish a focused collection of student writing once each year. The possibility for topics is endless. In the year of Vermont's bicentennial, we gathered and published a collection of oral histories from community members. When math portfolios first arrived, we published a math magazine including poems, problems, and stories about math. Once we documented a year of integrated units with a collection of topic-based poems. In response to an environmental unit, we created a field guide about our school's nature trail, including information about its several ecosystems, a map, and nature poems and drawings. The year Lincoln was hit with a major flood, the students wrote a collection of personal essays about their own experiences with the flood. These became part of a movement-based performance piece. In connection with our homes unit, we compiled a self-guided walking tour of ten historic homes in our community, including an extensively researched essay and a detailed, labeled sketch of each of the houses. As an added bonus, these publications were distributed in the community, helping to promote a positive image and an increased understanding of our program.

The Vermont Math Portfolio has promoted an increased emphasis on writing across the curriculum in our state. In fact, students eventually discover that the best write-ups to math and science problems are clear and concise, punctuated with strong visuals and mathematical or scientific equations. This same skill of focusing on precise language is useful in other content areas when students are asked to state the main idea or to summarize a passage.

Poetry exercises provide wonderful opportunities for students who may not excel in other areas of writing as a means to show deep levels of insight, sensitivity, and understanding in relation to topics of study. One year, for example, the students composed a wonderful collection of poems about the plight of characters they had come to know through our group readings about homelessness. Here is an example:

Clay's Hotel

I got out of bed,
expecting breakfast
but no one was there.
The room was silent
but outside sounded like a stuck jackhammer.
A carton of milk
sat on the counter.
It was empty.
I looked out the window.
Tall skyscrapers and burned out buildings
stood about.
I was lonely,
yearning for mom to come back.
I heard someone walking through the hallway . . .
Mom? I thought,
no.
It was just Mrs. Larkin and Jacob.

—Matthew Kimball

The students brought these poems to another level of expression by creating movement pieces to accompany them, in some cases adding musical effects as well. Their resulting presentation was quite effective and brought an emotional response from many viewers. To encourage this kind of result, it is important to ask students to place the same level of detail and focus in their poems that they put into other kinds of writing.

As mentioned in the introduction to this chapter, the stronger writers (often but not always the older ones) provide models for their peers in a multiage classroom. And students learn and polish their writing skills through ongoing sharing with and assistance from classmates.

Speaking

Speaking is the most fluid and natural form of communication for most students. It occurs in casual classroom conversations, in focused discussion, during student presentations or sharing, in theatrical exercises and performances, and during class meetings. The teacher's challenge lies in finding ways to promote learning through this readily available vehicle—in finding a balance between ongoing verbal distraction and rigidly controlled silence.

Many years ago, I volunteered in an intermediate classroom where the teacher dealt with this issue in a wonderful way. She established a clear set of expectations in the classroom depending upon the activity. During writing time, you could hear a pin drop. During cooperative group time, the classroom sounded like intermission at the theater. In both cases, students were completely involved in their work and produced superb results. This classroom became a model for me.

As I have evolved as a teacher, my perspective on the role of speaking in learning has also evolved. Now I look at the level of attention that students put into their discussions. I encourage students to explore their views through journal entries or by exchanging ideas with a partner before sharing with the larger group. In this way, students have the opportunity to develop a thought before expressing it more formally.

Authentic assessment has had the side benefit of promoting higher levels of reflective discussion among students during peer conferences. A few years ago, our class received a synthesizer and MIDI software setup as part of a statewide arts assessment program. For our unit on twentieth-century challenges, student pairs composed music relating to such themes as endangered plant species, deforestation, the Save the Whales campaign, drug use, and depletion of the ozone layer. Upon hearing each musical composition, students were asked to write a journal entry examining how well the music expressed its theme. Students were encouraged to include elements of music in their entries. The discussions that followed this guided writing were remarkably sophisticated.

In a similar fashion, the discussions we have about writing use the Vermont Writing Criteria as a framework. Students thus have a well-developed vocabulary for speaking about a topic that might otherwise prove elusive. One of the greatest academic gifts we can offer our students is to nurture the sort of expanded vocabulary that will, in turn, help them develop clear and precise thinking skills. The language of assessment is one of many effective ways to build vocabulary, both directly and indirectly.

Our performance of Shakespearean comedy expands my students' vocabulary in wonderful and unexpected directions. A number of students now quote Shakespeare in appropriate situations, and they also have a broader understanding of some of the origins of vernacular English.

One year our entire staff focused on listening and speaking skills through the theme of storytelling. We planned a series of engaging professional and student performances through which students gained an appreciation for the oral tradition, a tradition that doesn't always get equal time in our classrooms.

Class meetings provide further opportunity for students to practice the art of group conversation as students confront and discuss sometimes delicate topics among their peers, with a student or teacher acting as facilitator. Within this safe setting, students learn to express their ideas and opinions in a public forum.

Listening

It is often said that children have a short attention span. As noted earlier, I believe this is a profound misconception, easily disproved by the fact that children can engage in activities of personal interest for hours on end without a problem. When a child's attention is caught, he or she is as attentive as any other person. Hopefully, in such situations, there is something worthwhile to experience.

When I taught the primary grades, a parent approached me one day and asked if he could give a presentation to our class. He was willing to present on the topic of my choice. "I'm good at making complex things simple and interesting," he boasted. This parent, Jay, who was clearly successful in his field of technical sales, followed through splendidly on his offer. I suggested perhaps a thirty-minute presentation. My style of teaching isn't lecturing, and I wasn't sure how it would go over. Jay came in a few mornings later with some simple props and spoke for an hour and a half on atomic theory to my spellbound group of young learners. (I had told him that we were learning about matter.) I certainly could not have duplicated the performance, but it taught me something about children and their ability to listen.

On a more recent occasion, a friend loaned me an hour-long tape-recorded lecture presented by an expert on Shakespeare, our topic of study at that time. "You may want to share some selections on this tape with your students," she suggested. After listening to this captivating speaker, I decided there was nothing I could cut, so I played the entire tape for the class. My intermediate students showed that they could also focus and enjoy a lecture approach if given an outstanding presenter. In fact, at the end of the tape, my students requested an immediate repeat listening, to which I acquiesced and to which they listened with as much focus as the first playing. The information we gathered from this recording deepened our group understanding of Shakespeare and led to deeper levels of discussion.

Theater activities provide a playful context in which to practice listening skills. My husband, a theater major years ago, enjoys quoting one of his favorite pieces of advice about acting. "It's just listening and speaking, *listening* and *speaking*," a professor once told him. When I direct my students in a theatrical performance, I remind them that everyone on stage is acting, whether they are speaking or not. The responses of supporting actors provide much of the fuel for a powerful performance. These same listening skills, once developed, can be transferred to more mundane situations.

COOPERATIVE LEARNING AND LANGUAGE ARTS

Although most of the student writing that occurs in our class is composed individually, I also provide students with numerous opportunities for joint efforts. Students enjoy collaborating on creative writing, class presentations, playwriting, and research projects. While a close-knit pair of students will occasionally compose a wonderful poem that is a careful blending of the words of both authors, I generally request that students clearly define their roles in a collaborative project. In the case of a written final product of some length, I ask that each student be responsible for a particular section. This addresses the issue of accountability while also helping the students form a workable collaborative structure.

This system has not been foolproof. There have been instances when the materials handler lost the entire project folder the day before a month-long project was due or when one group member did not come through on her or his section. In general, though, the group will find its own standard and will request a consistent level of work from each of its members, even though some may need more support than others.

ASSESSING LANGUAGE ARTS

Language skills are assessed through a variety of tools. Spelling and vocabulary skills are evaluated both through traditional tests and in the context of usage. Students are encouraged to self-correct spelling by using the resources available to them: peers, dictionaries, word lists.

Writing is assessed through the aforementioned Vermont Writing Portfolio criteria. While it takes time and energy to internalize a set of standards such as the writing portfolio criteria, the results are worth it.

The feedback provided by a scored portfolio piece allows a student to pinpoint where there is room for improvement and where he or she is already strong.

Our school has begun to examine reading assessment more closely, and our early grades are participating in a Reading Recovery Program. This is an area relatively new to me. I have experimented with a form of modified miscue analysis in which the student reads a passage aloud, then answers a variety of questions to assess his or her comprehension of the passage. In this way, I can tally each student's decoding skills as well as her or his ability to follow a story line, gather information, make inferences, summarize the main idea, and synthesize and analyze information. This assessment takes me about fifteen minutes per student, though much time can be saved by asking students to write down answers to the questions. (An additional benefit of asking students to write answers is that a record of their responses can then be kept.) I carry out this assessment once per student during each of our three marking periods. I find it is most revealing if I use a reading with which the students and I are somewhat familiar.

Here are the sorts of questions I use with the students:

Decoding Skills

- Please read this passage. [Use passage on grade level.]

Follows Story Line

- What happened to Clay after his father left home?
- How is Clay's new apartment found?
- Where is the mother of the children Armand finds under the bridge?
- Where do the children meet before leaving for their journey West?

Gathers Information

- In what city and neighborhood is the park located?
- Why are children placed in foster homes, according to Mrs. Greg?
- Describe several challenges faced on the journey West.
- What have you found out about Paris from this story?

Makes Inferences

- What sort of person is Clay's mom?
- What is Armand implying when he turns down his friend's job offer?
- How do you know that Frances Mary has taken on her mother's role?
- How does Clay feel about the social worker?

Summarizes Main Idea

- Summarize this story in two sentences.
- What is this chapter about?
- What is this story about?

NOTE: A summary is not a retelling; it looks broadly at the plot to tell what the story is *about.*

Synthesizes and Analyzes

- Compare the two main characters in this story.
  - –How are they alike and different?
- Do you think the children's mother made a wise decision?
  - –Why or why not?
- Who is the bravest character in this story?
  - –Back up your answer with examples.
- What is the most significant event in this chapter?
  - –Back up your answer.
- What is the most significant event in this story?
  - –Back up your answer.

Finally, language arts are assessed through all the interactions I have with students throughout the day as well as my observations of their interactions with others.

SCHEDULING LANGUAGE ARTS

For a number of years, I have been able to schedule two additional staff members in my classroom once or twice each week. During this time period, we hold three simultaneous literature groups in which we generally work on three different group novels. As stated above, students complete reading assignments at home that involve reading, reflective writing, and their group role; I prepare an assignment packet for each group. The groups spend most of their time engaged in animated discussion. Remaining time is spent beginning the assignment for the following week. Students are also given thirty minutes of silent time on each of the other weekdays to work on reading goals.

Writing is formally scheduled for one hour each day. I request assistance for my needier students during this time block. While the use of classroom contracts allows students to arrange their own schedules, I request that this hour be a quiet work time so that students who write more fluidly in a calm environment will have this optimal setting provided for them.

Reading the student news periodical is a weekly homework assignment. When relevant topics arise, we discuss them during class time. I do not schedule a specific time for this purpose on a regular basis, though much informal discussion is sparked by the student magazine.

Word study is also a weekly homework assignment. A small amount of class time is devoted to spelling strategies and word study. I test students within their ability-level groups each Friday afternoon. Periodically, we work as a class on homophones or unit-based vocabulary. Vocabulary is also incorporated into reading assignments and all of the other subject areas.

ADAPTING TO VARIOUS NEEDS AND ABILITIES

Our reading groups are quite loosely divided according to ability levels, and I choose the readings accordingly. I might place a strong but reluctant reader with a group of slower readers; this student will frequently initiate a higher level of discussion among the students. One year I accidentally ended up with two groups divided by gender. Capitalizing on this division, I chose books with male or female protagonists according to each respective group, and it worked out splendidly. Sometimes, after hearing the excitement from their peers, a group will ask to read a book at the next level up for their second reading in a unit. In these ways, enthusiasm for reading can be generated among the groups. I try to make sure that all books I choose are well written and of high interest to my students. The pleasure in a book sparks a flame in the group, and this can inspire students to stretch their potentials. Given a poor choice, the opposite can also happen.

As mentioned previously, it is important for students who are weak in language arts to have the support they need to be successful. During our formal writing time, I try to have additional help available in the classroom. It is, of course, important that all adults working with students are clear on the given assignment. This can be presented either through the weekly student contracts or through a quick verbal interaction.

While our school uses a combination of pullout and in-class support, students in the upper-elementary grades tend to be more resistant to pullout programs that separate them from their peers. When it is determined that a student will be taken out of the classroom for the benefit of a more focused lesson, I always request that this occur at a time when we are working on the same subject area in class. If this is not possible, my second choice is to remove the student from a topic he/she would not benefit from due to his/her limitations.

Although we are a small school of about 120 students, we have begun taking a serious look at the needs of our more capable students. In reading groups, I always have several high-level novels and essay topics on hand so that students who are able to compact the assignment have someplace to go next. Unless a group leader is available, this works best on an individual basis. Our principal, who takes great interest in literature, has worked with small groups of accelerated students during lunchtime or even during our scheduled group reading times. The students respond enthusiastically to this sort of enrichment.

In the area of writing, even within the confines of a particular assignment, I find that I can set expectations and provide feedback according to the needs and abilities of my individual students. When I am fortunate to have a classroom aide available, the needier students receive additional support. At other times, particularly with weaker students who also have attention deficits, I sometimes request the aid of parents in helping their child get caught up over the weekend. This also provides an opportunity to join with the family in supporting a particular student. (For this reason, the only assignment I give on Fridays is to get caught up on missed work.)

MULTIAGE CONSIDERATIONS

Because our language arts program is closely linked with the content areas and with social studies in particular, the multiyear curriculum follows naturally from unit themes. There is a higher-cost factor involved in planning for two or three years of trade books as opposed to just one. This amount is multiplied if a teacher chooses to develop new or adapted units periodically. This factor alone provides a strong incentive for the concept of teaming or at least of sharing materials across classrooms or even among schools. When teachers and administrators are receptive to this possibility, it can lead to a fertile exchange of ideas while saving thousands of dollars.

In terms of the students themselves, it can be challenging to provide language arts assignments that appeal to a group that is crossing developmental lines. For example, in my grades 5/6 class, some of the students have preadolescent interests in romance and social cliques, while others remain interested in such topics as pets and best friends. This has not been a huge issue, though it tends to get emphasized at the end of the school year, when sixth graders look toward middle school and making the break from elementary school. On the bright side, the combination of fifth and sixth graders helps inhibit many of the difficult issues that can arise in a straight sixth-grade classroom.

5

MULTIAGE SOCIAL STUDIES

Renaissance music spills across the room. The stage is set with a semicircle of painted backdrops, a potted tree, a silver stool, and a Greek pillar. The audience completes the circle to form a broadly defined facsimile of the Globe Theatre. In the pause after the music, the spectators wait in anticipation. Soon the Duke of Athens and Queen Hippolyta stride out bedecked in silver and golden crowns and flowing robes. *A Midsummer Night's Dream* begins.

As Shakespeare's sinuous story unfolds, the stage is filled with royalty and lovers, fools and fairies. Titania is a proud fairy queen, Oberon is brash but compassionate, and Puck is full of mischief. The fairies sparkle with their magic. The thespians are foolish and silly, and Nick Bottom is the most outlandish of all. Each student is immersed in his or her role. Certain students clearly have a passion and talent for theater; all of them have come to embrace their characters.

THE CULMINATING EVENT IN
A UNIT ON THE RENAISSANCE

This presentation of *A Midsummer Night's Dream* was the culminating event of a classroom unit on the European Renaissance in which particular emphasis was placed on Elizabethan England and the Shakespearean theater. The class researched and analyzed major events that occurred during this time period and read novels about the spread of ideas and knowledge through travel during the sixteenth century. They studied the life of William Shakespeare and the culture surrounding his Globe Theatre. Upon learning that Shakespearean actors were sometimes pelted with tomatoes by an unsatisfied audience, the class was determined to hold the attention of their viewers. (Tomatoes were considered poisonous in Elizabethan times.)

A huge amount of learning takes place in the process of preparing a class play. Students become so interested in Shakespearean theater that they sit spellbound through a tape-recorded lecture by Professor Elliot Engel from the University of North Carolina and immediately request a rerun of the entire tape. In his lecture, Professor Engel discusses such topics as the very conscious evolution of the British accent (over 100 years after Shakespeare's death), the origin of the term "box office" (the place where boxes of coins were locked up at the Globe Theatre), and the nature of Shakespeare's original audiences (most were illiterate street workers).

After roles are assigned in the play, time is spent reading and discussing the play line by line. Once students thoroughly understand the plot and their individual parts, they explore the body language and voices of their respective characters so that lines can be presented in a way that will help the audience make sense of them. As students become comfortable with their individual roles, they begin to unfold the comical and surprising relationships among the various characters throughout the play. All the while, they are learning how to speak in front of a group.

Class parents and community members assist students with rehearsals, set construction, costumes, makeup, and music. High school students enrolled in local performing arts and video technology programs provide lighting and record a videotape of the production.

It is delightful to see such pleasure in the eyes of a youthful audience as Puck and Oberon play with the hearts of Titania and four Athenian lovers, fairies flit around a transformed Nick Bottom, and a troupe of would-be actors stumble over one another. As for the students (to paraphrase the words of Shakespeare), the truth be known, they are merry as the day is long and ready to make the world their stage.

THE VALUE OF THEATER ARTS IN A MULTIAGE SOCIAL STUDIES PROGRAM

Much has been written in recent years about the value of simulations in studying social studies topics. Theatrical events serve a similar function, allowing students to delve into another culture or time period and providing multidimensional experiential learning. In producing a Renaissance play—complete with a full stage set, Renaissance music, elaborate costumes, Shakespearean quotes hung on the walls, and an illuminated WELCOME sign at the entrance to the performance hall— students learn much about Shakespearean language and Elizabethan traditions.

Theatrical productions are an outstanding vehicle that can be adapted to the needs and abilities of individuals. When a script is chosen or created so that it provides interesting roles for numerous students, it is possible to cast students accordingly. I allow the students to decide how many lines they feel comfortable memorizing. Then, after a bit of negotiation with a few students who underestimate their own abilities, I assign roles.

A class play is also a wonderful opportunity to enhance group cohesion and enrich the classroom culture. Students remark on how much they enjoyed working with one another, and the script encourages students to interact with one another in new ways.

There are also options for classroom productions that do not involve a formal script. With younger students, I frequently adapt an interesting folktale to create a class play. One or two narrators can fill in details left out by the actors. Another possibility is for students to create their own script. This, of course, adds time to the unit, but students have an opportunity to develop their creative and literary abilities as playwrights. The addition of an artist-in-residence can add greatly to the experience. Here are a few ideas I've tried for student-created productions:

- For a unit on Greek mythology, student groups each present a myth. This can also be done effectively as a puppet show.
- For a unit on African Americans, students create reader's theater pieces about historic figures.
- A medieval festival is a great way to conclude a unit on the Middle Ages. Student groups perform as jesters, troubadours, actors, jugglers, jousters, musicians, and dancers. This provides options for students with unique skills and abilities.
- For a unit on diversity and adversity in the twentieth century, student groups each portray a cultural group or subculture and the challenges it faced during a particular decade, including music and even a dance from that period.

- For a unit on local history, student groups each portray a time period from the past. These can be based on oral histories and local documents.
- When focusing on a time period in American history, the class can create a collaborative fictional narrative based on actual historic events, develop it into a script, and produce it as a play. (We did this over a three-month period with the support of a playwright through an arts grant.)

Sometimes it's valuable to explore whether our deeply held beliefs line up with current reality. With this in mind, upon completing our production of *Twelfth Night* last March, I asked students to respond to a survey on its personal value as a learning experience. The results, quite appropriately, were dramatic. Students were in unanimous agreement that the production was important to their growth, but the reasons they gave were diverse. They mentioned learning how to express their feelings, present themselves to an audience, overcome stage fright, use their bodies for self-expression, project and articulate, memorize lines, work closely with others who aren't part of their circle of friends, wait to speak, listen actively, concentrate, organize, and understand Shakespeare's language and time period, as well as realizing "that patience and lots of hard work pays off.". When students were asked what they learned about themselves through this experience, their responses included the following remarks:

I have talent I didn't know I had.
I can do something if I try really hard at it.
I learned not to be afraid to speak up.
I learned how to work with other people.
I can change to be something else.
I can perform in front of an audience.
I learned not to be embarrassed in front of an audience, to always believe in myself and don't give up.
I learned to be more self-confident.
I can do anything if I focus and work hard enough
I can be anything in the world I want to be.

These words affirmed my belief that classroom theatrical productions have the potential to encompass both the mandated curriculum and the child's own implicit agenda as an emerging social individual.

ASPECTS OF A MULTIAGE
SOCIAL STUDIES PROGRAM

There is a general format that I use for the development of most social studies units. Initially, I look for one or more outstanding teacher's guides and a collection of student resources relating to the unit's topic. I frequently use curriculum materials designed for gifted and talented students, because I find they offer exciting and stimulating activities and encourage independent study. Whenever possible, I also gather several student novels for reading groups and a read-aloud novel that relate to the theme. (The reading component of the unit was discussed in chapter 4.)

To begin the unit in class, we discuss what students already know about the topic, and I ask what students would like to learn so they can begin to think toward their independent study project. Next, students often carry out mini-research projects on a list of topics related to the theme. If we are discussing an historical time period, the list may result in a timeline of short essays accompanied by illustrations. Other topics, such as the study of local architecture, may involve researching a list of basic concepts. This work is completed in a couple of days and serves as an overview of the unit.

Occasionally, we use the students' list of initial questions about the topic as a focus for our mini-research. Usually, however, I create the list to assure a broad foundation of information. Students present their mini-research findings to one another and display them on a bulletin board as a reference throughout the unit.

Once students have some basic information, I often show them a videotape about the topic, which reinforces their basic knowledge. Using this sequence, I find that students are able to appreciate a video that may be considered appropriate for older students, especially if it is not too long and we discuss information that may be problematic.

At this point, I generally assign a collection of readings and activities gleaned from the curriculum materials I have gathered. This allows students to become more immersed in the subject area and opens the possibility for some in-depth discussions among students. In reading about Elizabethan England, for example, the class became quite intrigued with the infamous Henry VIII and the irony that his heir, a woman, became perhaps the most famous ruler in British history. As we read about the Globe Theatre, students became curious and fascinated to learn about the nature of Shakespeare's audiences, the rowdy events that sometimes unfolded at his performances, and Shakespeare's ability to entertain a broad range of people with his literary and theatrical genius.

The activities assigned at this point in the unit generally involve a variety of intelligences. Students solve puzzles, build models and posters, create and view artwork and music, write poems and lyrics, and gather more information about subtopics of interest. This is where I depend heavily on the use of well-designed materials that spark students' interest while engaging them with rich content. It is important to use activities that help students examine and consider unit concepts from both a concrete and an analytical perspective. They might be asked to consider, for instance, how an important historic event or individual would be viewed today. This interpretation might be expressed in a newspaper editorial, in new lyrics to a popular song, or through a short dramatic skit.

Depending on the unit timeline, we have several options at this point. Students can choose an independent project that will be presented in a format of their own design for the culminating event of the unit. We may decide to produce a play, performance, or festival as the culminating event, and we will spend the duration of the unit working on our individual roles. Or, if the unit has a cross-curricular focus for several months, we may decide to do both independent projects and a group presentation.

INDEPENDENT PROJECTS IN A MULTIAGE SOCIAL STUDIES PROGRAM

As students get older, it is important that they be asked to choose projects with an increasingly defined focus. While a seven-year-old might be interested in learning about castles, for example, an upper-elementary student could be asked to compare French and English castles during the Middle Ages or to discuss the way of life defined by castles.

When introducing a project, I start by stating my goals and expectations, and then we discuss the range of possible products. Then the students and I work together to define expected outcomes, along with a scoring guide (described more specifically in the upcoming section on assessment) and a project timeline that defines when each portion is due. I post the scoring guide and timeline in the classroom, and we discuss student progress each day.

RESEARCH SKILLS, CONCEPTS, AND COOPERATIVE LEARNING IN SOCIAL STUDIES UNITS

Social studies units about foreign cultures and historic time periods involve an understanding of many abstract concepts. Skills involved in gathering, analyzing, and sharing such concepts include reading, note taking, writing, listening, speaking and discussing, mapping, sketching, and observing. Students who excel in one or more of these areas have the opportunity to exercise and develop their strengths.

There are many fine teacher resources that help students develop research skills. Even so, special needs students can find themselves at a loss. For this reason, I try to recruit assistance from specialists and/or aides for these students with unit concepts and research projects. While stronger students can help the others, I do not rely on them to support students in need of considerable attention. This is the time when all students are best empowered to reach to their highest limits, and I don't want any of them to feel held back.

Nevertheless, my students generally enjoy working with a partner on their projects, and this allows them to build on their individual skills. Social studies projects lend themselves well to cooperative learning, especially when roles and expectations are clearly defined. Once again, I have found that strong curriculum materials help clarify these areas. With projects that are more loosely defined, I ask students to work alone or in pairs, where it is up to them to define the parameters of the task. In paired groups, I generally allow students to choose their own partners, though I retain veto power and request that they rotate through a number of partners during the course of the year.

INTEGRATING LANGUAGE ARTS WITH THE SOCIAL STUDIES CURRICULUM

For students to develop a sophisticated understanding of social studies topics, it is essential that they be able to gather and interpret information in a variety of formats, much of it language based. Therefore, we generally pair our social studies unit with our language arts program.

As mentioned above, students often begin the unit with several language arts activities, discussing what they already know about the topic and then completing mini-research projects in which they seek information in resource books and on the Web. Of course, this introduction also includes audiovisual information.

In many units, students are asked to complete creative writing assignments to develop their impressions of the topic. During our Renaissance unit, each student wrote a story set in Renaissance times. Students spent several weeks developing the characters, setting, and plot before actually drafting their stories and conferencing with peers. I observed that this preparatory work enabled students to exercise more control than they usually exhibit in a longer piece of creative writing. This extended exercise also helped them develop a feeling for the time period we were studying. Revised final drafts were scored according to the Vermont Writing Portfolio criteria.

Students are encouraged to present independent research projects in a variety of formats, including posters and artwork, puppet shows, dramatic presentations, student-made videos, and hands-on demonstrations. Even so, the language component remains a central factor as students seek alternate means to gather and share their information.

Composing and presenting a performance, while involving many modes of learning, is also a language-based experience. In the case of a formal play, for example, students memorize and deliver a series of lines. To do this effectively, it is also essential that they understand the context and meaning of their spoken words in terms of the broader plot and historic implications. This is always a key factor in preparing a Shakespearean production.

As mentioned in chapter 4, well-selected novels for the group can also enhance a social studies unit, providing students with an internal picture and feeling for an issue or time period outside of their personal experience.

ASSESSING SOCIAL STUDIES PROJECTS: ALTERNATIVE AND TRADITIONAL ROUTES

As in other areas of the curriculum, I assess students in social studies in a variety of ways. Each assessment tool is adapted to the learning goal in question.

Social studies projects offer wonderful opportunities for new forms of assessment that consider how students can apply and synthesize their knowledge instead of just measuring the facts they can recall.

Students can even take part in defining the criteria by which they will be assessed and in evaluating their own work. This can be done while maintaining high expectations and while remaining faithful to state and local standards. The criteria are developed and presented along with the assignment so that students know at the outset how their work will be evaluated. My colleagues and I find that students strive to create their best work when they understand and appreciate assessment criteria.

To spark students' interest, build on their strengths, and adapt to various learning styles, I offer students an array of possibilities for their independent projects. In a unit on Greek mythology, for example, the students were asked to retell a classic myth in one of a variety of formats. They could present it as an illustrated children's story, an epic poem, a work of visual art, an interpretive dance with musical accompaniment, a story in the oral tradition with sound and/or musical effects, a reader's theater piece, a puppet show, a video, or a dramatic skit.

At the outset of the project, the students and I discuss the criteria by which the final product will be assessed. A theatrical performance is assessed according to standards for use of voice and awareness of audience and character. Written work is assessed by the Vermont Writing Portfolio criteria, with which my students are all familiar. It is also assessed, along with the presentation portion, according to how well it meets what we define as the social studies project goals. Here are some criteria we might choose for the Greek myth project (note that we consider both group and individual efforts):

- The work represents its respective Greek myth with *accuracy* and *detail.*
- The work effectively represents its respective myth to an audience; it is *organized* and *well rehearsed.*
- The student worked *collaboratively* and *cooperatively* with his/her group.
- The student was *focused* and *well prepared* for his/her role in the project.

Here is another set of criteria that we created for a generic independent project:

●●●

SPECIAL PROJECT EVALUATION FORM

NAME:

FINAL PRODUCTS SUBMITTED: 6 PTS. EACH

___REPORT
___VISUAL
___PRESENTATION
___RESEARCH

REPORT   5 PTS. EACH

___MAINTAINS FOCUS ON QUESTION
___ORGANIZED, CLEAR WRITING
___INCLUDES APPROPRIATE DETAIL
___APPROPRIATE VOICE AND TONE
___GRAMMAR, USAGE, AND MECHANICS

VISUAL   5 PTS. EACH

___FOCUSES ON QUESTION / INCLUDES APPROPRIATE INFORMATION
___DESIGN AND VISUAL IMPACT
___LABELED APPROPRIATELY
___CORRECT AND WELL-RESEARCHED INFORMATION

PRESENTATION   5 PTS. EACH

___SHOWS UNDERSTANDING OF TOPIC AND ISSUES INVOLVED IN
   QUESTION
___SHOWS PREPARATION AND ORGANIZATION
___SPEAKS CLEARLY TO AUDIENCE
___PRESENTED IN A CREATIVE OR INTERESTING FORMAT

RESEARCH   10 PTS

___INCLUDES SEVERAL APPROPRIATE RESOURCES

GOODWILL   1 FREE POINT!

___

EXTRA CREDIT   UP TO 10 PTS.   SPECIFY WORK:

___WORK BEYOND REQUIREMENTS OF PROJECT

TOTAL POINTS:

●●●

For each of these criteria, students are scored along a continuum. We spend time discussing the range in quality for each criterion, though we don't always take the time to create a full rubric. Rather, the students set standards for themselves and one another. Generally, I ask students to score their own work before they see my assessment of it. It is interesting to observe that many students are quite clear on their own strengths and weaknesses.

Traditional short essay tests are an effective way to assess how knowledgeable students have become about the terms, concepts, and details of a thematic unit in the social studies. I usually give students a review guide that we discuss in class, and their results on these short essay tests are generally excellent. I have noticed, however, that some students can be very good at memorizing information without really understanding it. The stronger students stand out on such tests, because they tend to assimilate the information and articulate it in a more thoughtful manner. At any rate, objective tests give all students a feeling that they have accomplished a body of learning. Used in conjunction with observations and the sort of assessment tools mentioned above that look at the bigger picture, they are part of an effective assessment program.

Several years ago, I stumbled across a means of assessment not ordinarily used with students in the intermediate grades. Our marking period ended three days after we returned from the February break, and we were into the last week of rehearsals for our class Shakespearean production. To avoid the added pressure on students of studying for a test, I decided to try an open-book test. The results were revealing.

The big question was: Define the European Renaissance. After that, the students were given five categories of activity, including science and invention, government and politics, trade and exploration, arts and culture, and religion. Using our initial timeline research and any books in our classroom, students were asked to provide three examples of specific events that fit into each category. Points were given for explaining the significance of each event. Students could discuss this information with anyone, including me, but they had to write down the information in their own words. For bonus points, they could select and defend one event as the most significant of the time period.

Initially, many students thought this test was a breeze, but they soon discovered that it wasn't as easy as they'd thought. Close to half of the class failed the test. I gave those students another day to work on it in class, and the scores all went up as students came to understand what they were being asked to do. This test led to some of the more focused and in-depth discussions of our unit.

One particularly bright student remarked, "This test is actually helping me learn. We should do more of these." I realized that I hadn't been asking my students to do enough analytical thinking on their assessments. Now I push them to apply the concepts we've studied to novel situations and to view them in broader contexts.

Recently, I've experimented with the use of focusing questions as a means of assessment. Focusing questions, which target a unit of study on a specific learning standard or set of standards, also help define the work as an inquiry. Big questions can be carried through a unit and turned back to students at the conclusion for a challenging open-ended form of assessment. For example, in a study of Canada's geography, we focused on the question: What factors impacted settlement and migration patterns in Canada? Asking students to address this question on their own after completing the unit gave me a direct window into what each individual internalized with regard to the standard.

FRAMING THE TIME: SCHEDULING SOCIAL STUDIES

Current literature touts the value of extended learning periods. I couldn't agree more. For years I have lobbied for uninterrupted time in my classroom, and I continue to arrange my schedule to provide for this preference. I request special subjects, such as art and physical education, at the very beginning or end of the morning or afternoon so that the rest of our time can be open.

Our multiage program has experimented with several different scheduling models in social studies. During my first several years at my present school, I teamed with another class for science and social studies. We had a daily ninety-minute time block in which we engaged in one unit of study, alternating the focus between science and social studies.

I currently work in a self-contained classroom, where we devote about ninety minutes each afternoon to science and social studies unit work. Significant writing projects are carried out during our morning writer's workshop, the quiet work period when we frequently have the support of a paraprofessional to assist students with language difficulties. More active learning occurs in the afternoon.

That is our formal schedule. In fact, because we use a contract system in our classroom, students carry out assignments throughout the day.

When I assign a social studies project in the students' contracts, I let them know how much time I think it will take them to complete it thoroughly, and students schedule their time accordingly. Of course, there are occasions when we need to coordinate our time as a class for cooperative projects, group presentations, or play rehearsals, and these are generally scheduled into our afternoon block.

ADAPTATIONS IN THE MULTIAGE SOCIAL STUDIES CLASSROOM: A CHALLENGE FOR ALL

Through the use of art, drama, music, models, design projects, and simulations, it is possible to adapt social studies projects to the needs, abilities, and interests of a variety of students. When choices are available, I find that students tend to choose options that suit them, though I encourage students to reach higher or adjust their goals as I observe the need. If an adept student has completed his/her assignment well in advance, I may suggest adding a computerized graph or map, interviewing a local expert, or delving deeper into a specific subtopic. Another student may need reinforcement with central concepts and issues. I generally assist this student in sorting and organizing his/her ideas to apply them to the task at hand. For example, I might work with such a student to create a conceptual map of the assignment so that the student has a better idea of where he/she is going with it. At other times, I might go through a small portion of the task with the student, reducing concepts to their least common denominator and encouraging the student to verbalize the steps involved in carrying out the work. Sometimes it is helpful to reinforce a key concept with the entire class through carefully designed concrete learning experiences.

As mentioned above, there is one potential area of challenge in exploring social studies topics with students of greatly divergent abilities. Language and conceptual skills are integral to social studies, and students with gaps in these areas will need additional support. This is where I recruit the assistance of our special education and Title I teams. They provide assistance in the form of in-class support, on-level research materials, and pullout tutorials. Although in-class options are generally better received by students, the pullout option allows the special educator to design an alternate group project and follow through with an individual or small group in a calm workspace. As pointed out previously, this can yield high-quality, optimal student learning.

With traditional tests, I may assess a student orally if he/she is having considerable difficulty with a written test. Alternative assessment tools tend to work well with students of all levels.

CREATING A SOCIAL STUDIES PROGRAM FOR THE MULTIAGE CLASSROOM: THE BIG PICTURE

I have barely scratched the surface of outstanding possibilities in creating a challenging, exciting, and developmentally appropriate multiage social studies program. Fortunately, many fine resources already exist, including the national standards for history, geography, and social studies, as well as topic-specific curriculum guides that are frequently designed to address a spectrum of grade levels. The broad subject area of social studies is perhaps the most readily adaptable to a multiage setting, particularly by an educator who is already comfortable teaching to multiple intelligences and a variety of learning styles.

In creating a two- or three-year curriculum plan, a school may want to consider designing a sequence of units that build on one another, recognizing that students will enter the sequence at various stages. Our intermediate program initially created a three-year plan that moves historically. Although, as explained in chapter 2, this overview has since evolved, our plan was originally sequenced as follows:

Year One	Year Two	Year Three
History of the Universe	Ancient Civilizations	American Studies
Earth's History	Middle Ages/Renaissance	
Early Humans	Vermont Studies	

Whatever the details, a carefully thought-out plan allows for connections across topics of study, resulting in a valuable synthesis of information and experiences. In this way, students move toward the goal of social studies education, acquiring a broad understanding of the relationships between humans and our physical and cultural worlds. Grasping these relationships gives students greater insights into both their own lives and other subjects in the school curriculum.

THOUGHTS ON THE CHANGING FACE OF SOCIAL STUDIES

National standards in the social studies now require elementary teachers to place greater emphasis on underlying conceptual themes when addressing a unit of study. This represents a shift from a more topic-centered approach and requires a deeper level of understanding and planning on the part of classroom teachers. Social studies units need to be reworked or even redesigned to address specific standards.

For example, a year ago, we adapted our unit on twentieth-century America. At first, this unit focused on the major events of each decade. Referring to the standards, we came up with a more specific and unified focus: "Diversity and Adversity in the Twentieth-Century United States." We presented this unit to our students in the form of a focusing question: How have our diverse backgrounds influenced our varied experiences as Americans in the twentieth century? After a great deal of planning, gathering of materials, and refining things along the way, we came up with a remarkable learning experience for both teachers and students.

This project involved our two intermediate multiage classrooms. We spent the first several weeks grasping an overview of the major events of the twentieth century, then dove into the nitty-gritty of nine issues various groups faced throughout the past 100 years, addressing such topics as immigration through Ellis Island, child labor at the turn of the century, the struggle for women's suffrage, and Japanese American internment during World War II. Student groups each researched one of these issues; then students wrote personal essays in the voice of a child experiencing the issue. Eventually, each group of four or five students collaborated on a scene to depict their research, drawing content from their essays and primary or secondary sources. The collection of scenes was melded together with musical accompaniment for each group's portrayal, performed by students and teachers. The full work, framed in a choral reading composed by the students, had a powerful impact. At the end of the unit, every student had a sense of the challenging role of diversity in our evolving nation during the twentieth century.

While certainly time-consuming, this sort of in-depth and focused unit bears wonderful fruit in a multiage classroom, where student leaders have been cultivated and where the learning is carried forward into a second year, providing further opportunities for reflection and growth. For instance, a certain line from one of the skits became a classroom refrain the following year, and students looked back to their roles as reference points in their personal and academic development. Such comments as "I'm not as frightened to speak on stage as I was in our last play" or "That reminds me of the people in internment camps we read about last year" affirm the significance of this carryover.

6

MULTIAGE SCIENCE

A unit on sound in our 5/6 class yields the following endeavors:

Mary and Meredith, two alert sixth graders, sit at a computer attached to a simple oscilloscope. They are among the first students to use this instrument. Mary hums into its microphone, varying her vocal pattern from high to low and from loud to soft.

"Wow, that screechy sound made a wild pattern!" Meredith giggles as Mary attempts to repeat it.

When Mary is pleased with the effect, she gives Meredith a signal to record her sound on the computer. Then they reverse roles. The result is two sound wave patterns displayed on the computer screen. After printing the patterns, the two girls discuss possible reasons for the various heights and lengths of waves, jotting down some sketches and notes in their science journals.

"Tomorrow, let's bring in our instruments and see what kind of wave patterns they make," Meredith suggests. Since Mary and Meredith are known for their abilities on the clarinet and the flute, respectively, other students take note of Meredith's suggestion. They are anxious to see what will happen tomorrow.

Next week all partners will be asked to choose one pair of wave patterns from their work on the computer to analyze in a formal write-up that addresses the basic sound concepts we've been discussing.

Meredith and Mary have played a subtle leadership role in modeling this activity.

Melissa, a fifth-grade student with special needs in language but a strong aptitude for science, has a plastic ruler. Holding the ruler down with one hand and flicking it with the other, she vibrates the ruler over the side of her desk like a little diving board. She asks Des to read her the next step in the lab. Des patiently puts her work aside to read to her friend and then returns to her own work. The instructions ask Melissa to repeat the activity, lengthening and shortening the amount of the ruler that hangs over the table.

"Oh, I get it!" she exclaims. "The sounds get lower when the ruler gets longer."

Melissa continues through the rest of the lab and then begins her write-up. She asks Des to help her with a number of words along the way. Although Des is in the same grade as Melissa, she is taking a helping role typically seen in a multiage classroom.

Chris, a sixth grader, is putting his final touches on a poster about sound safety. A strong visual artist, he has divided the poster into two sections, one with drawings of dangerous practices, the other with safer procedures. He includes images of a tractor, a lawn mower, and some other heavy machinery. On one side, there is a person wearing headphones. On the other side, a cartoon character stands at tense attention, eyes bugging out. Chris is working on labeling the poster with the kinds of sounds that push the limits of safety. Sitting beside him is a younger student, immersed in a project of his own, who periodically gazes admiringly over to Chris's artwork.

"Most people don't realize that even a loud lawn mower can damage your hearing," Chris explains to me when I stop by his desk.

In the meantime, other students are absorbed in projects of their own. Ruth is meeting with our principal, a concert musician. She is creating a graph depicting the musical range of various instruments. Wayne has been reading about the speech and hearing ranges of various animals, and he is deciding how to present this information.

Everyone in the class is creating stories in which sound has an impact. They incorporate magical sounds, unusual sounds, never-been-heard-before sounds, and sound signals. Each story is imaginative, but some are especially effective. Brian, an extremely active sixth grader, creates a world in which sound does not exist, painting a rich picture of what that might be like. Then, in the middle of the story, sound is introduced to this world by a strange visitor. Brian envisions all the wonderful and difficult results of introducing sound into a world of silence.

When the stories are complete, we hold a class reading. Students enjoy commenting on the writing of their peers, encouraging their abilities in focus, organization, voice and tone, and details. Later in the year or even in the following year, Brian's theme will likely emerge in the work of a younger writer who was captured by his older classmate's fantasy.

Other activities in our sound unit include additional hands-on experiments that explore the nature of sound, journal entries that discuss and analyze experiments, a CD that demonstrates hundreds of instruments and musical styles, electronic musical composition using our MIDI lab, original poems accompanied with musical effects, a Bill Nye science video on sound, and ongoing discussions about basic sound concepts and terminology. Together, these experiences help students expand and develop their understanding of the principles of sound and its impact on our lives. More broadly speaking, the students develop scientific skills and concepts that they can apply to future learning.

ASPECTS OF A MULTIAGE SCIENCE PROGRAM

Our science curriculum is similar to what you might find in a single-grade classroom, although we work within a multiyear framework. Over the course of two or three years in our classroom, a student will explore the science concepts designated by national, state, and local standards for the relevant grade levels. We fit these into a series of units as depicted in previous chapters.

A science topic can be presented in any of several formats—as a stand-alone science unit, as an integrated science unit, or as a component of a cross-curricular theme. A stand-alone science unit is focused primarily on the areas of science and math. A few years ago, our class did a mini-unit on pendulums. Students worked in cooperative groups to carry out a series of hands-on activities that involved creating, observing, timing, recording, analyzing, and theorizing about pendulums. This unit lasted one month, culminating with the creation of a ceiling-to-floor sand pendulum that drew wonderful patterns on a large black sheet of paper on the floor as a group of mesmerized students watched from the periphery. While this unit incorporated some math, reading, and writing skills, the focus was distinctly on science concepts.

An integrated science unit is one in which the focus is on a science topic, but activities are consciously spread across the curriculum. Our sound unit, depicted above, is an example of such an approach. The activities described incorporate science, math, technology, art, creative and expository writing, music appreciation and composition, research and interviewing skills, and public speaking. This unit lasted a full marking period and was the focus of our entire curriculum during this time. It culminated with an open house at which we displayed examples of student work, experiments for parents to try, and a videotape of student presentations on their independent projects.

Each fall we also present a unit in which science is one component of a cross-curricular theme. One year our theme was "Home, Architecture, and Structure," an elaborate unit described in detail in chapter 8. Another year our fall theme was "Space." We studied the science of rocketry, focusing on Newton's laws as we carried out a series of design tasks that involved building, testing, and analyzing a variety of rocket-powered vehicles. These activities, one of which is described at the start of chapter 2, involved lots of math/science integration. A rocket scientist visited our class and spoke with us about the principles of rocket fuel. In social studies, we examined the history, development, and impact of the space program. Students mapped the solar system and the constellations and carried out math activities dealing with astronomical distances, planetary sizes in relation to gravity, and distances between planets and the sun. For language arts, the class read and wrote science fiction stories as well as folklore about the night sky. Each student also wrote a poem about a particular planet or star, combining science with mythology. Accompanying each poem was a NASA image, manipulated by the students through an image-processing program.

SKILLS AND CONCEPTS:
A CONSTRUCTIVIST/DISCOVERY APPROACH

One tendency in working on science concepts with students with a broad range of abilities is to place all the emphasis on hands-on experiences. This is likely to involve all students. However, current research points out that students are liable to draw many different conclusions from their experiences, some of which can lead to erroneous mental models of the way the scientific world works. For example, a colleague of mine offered what seemed like a straightforward experience to her grades 1/2 multiage students. She darkened the room and shone a flashlight; her purpose was to show the students that dust particles are everywhere around us. Her students drew quite a different conclusion: they decided that dust particles are attracted to light. Because this teacher's students were asked to discuss and write about their conclusions, she was able to catch this misconception and help them correct it.

As educators, we need to be sure that our students are asked to make scientific sense out of their experiences, and we may need to guide them in appropriate directions through follow-up activities. For this reason, we follow lab work with journal writing and guided discussion. The journal entries allow me to assess how well individuals grasp skills and concepts; guided discussion allows me to read the pulse of the group while helping students build their knowledge and arrive at central concepts. I spend further time with individuals and small groups who need more support and additional hands-on experiences to reinforce or correct conceptual understanding.

RESEARCH SKILLS AND CLASSROOM EXPERTS

Research projects can reinforce science concepts by providing students with the opportunity to seek and gather information about a subtopic of interest. As a side benefit, a classroom of experts emerges who will share their budding knowledge and enthusiasm with one another. Acknowledging individual strengths in science is another way to provide students with a meaningful academic role that helps them feel positive about school and themselves. A student who was knowledgeable about hamsters, for instance, took charge of our classroom pet one year. A mechanically inclined student helped out with our bottle rocket launchpad and reminded others of safety guidelines when tools were in use. In the primary grades, there is always a dinosaur or truck expert in the crowd. A multiage classroom is a wonderful place to nurture the cultivation of mastery, encouraging students to hone their interests, questions, and skills over a period of several years.

In a multiage classroom, there also tends to be several students who arise each year as scientific spokespersons for the group, frequently articulating insights a step or two ahead of the others. These scientifically inclined students, who may struggle in other academic areas, are prone to ask the sort of insightful questions we seek to encourage in our students. In doing so, they inspire their peers and help push the group learning curve in a positive direction.

MATH AND TECHNOLOGY AS COMPONENTS OF THE SCIENCE PROGRAM

The use of technological tools adds excitement and complexity to a science program. Our intermediate students have extended their learning in science through simulations, synthesizers, hypermedia stacks, CD-ROM and on-line research, scientific calculators, spreadsheet and geography software, telecommunications links with other classrooms, Lego/Logo projects, data analysis, and the use of scientific sensors that graph sound and movement. As pointed out earlier, the multiage classroom is an ideal environment in which to promote technological abilities, because student skills are passed along from year to year, thus making it possible to keep pace with evolving technologies.

Mathematics and science reinforce each other, particularly in the areas of statistics, measurement, and geometry. A number of years ago, we created a block in our day called the "math/science lab," and this project has continued to evolve. Students frequently complete portfolio problems that blend math and science skills. When we studied geology, for example, the students baked a three-layer corn bread. For their write-up, they were asked to determine why the layers separated and how that explanation might relate to the layers in the Earth. This problem involved an understanding of measurement, density, weight, solutions, liquids, and solids. A structural design task in an architecture unit led us into a discussion about the stability of various shapes. Our rocketry experiments involved the students with weighing, measuring, timing, recording, charting, graphing, analyzing, and interpreting data. Once again, older students who were more proficient in these skills took a leadership role, and all students benefited.

SCIENCE ASSESSMENT IN THE MULTIAGE CLASSROOM

Students are assessed in a variety of ways: through their journal entries and more formal portfolio write-ups, through their independent projects, and through tests on the concepts and vocabulary of the unit.

Just as in the social studies, specific criteria are defined for assessing journals, write-ups, and projects. Students are frequently involved in the development of these criteria, and they are always aware of them at the beginning of the project. I generally ask students to score their work before I do, and because they are clear about the criteria, they are also clear about the quality of their own and one another's work. The most conscientious students will revise their work further after they have scored it and before submitting it to me. Once a student submits a high-scoring journal entry, that piece becomes a personal benchmark for future entries. As a boy in my class stated, "I always use this for a model because it got me a five."

Occasionally, I vary test expectations according to grade and ability levels. For example, sixth graders might need to identify twenty local minerals, but the fifth graders would need to identify only fifteen. Inevitably, some fifth graders will want to show me that they can do sixth-grade-level work, and they will go for the twenty (and, generally, a bright sixth grader will lobby at class meeting to make sure that fifth graders do not have a higher potential score than sixth graders). In a quieter way, I will adjust the expectations for individual students having difficulty with memorization or the skills being assessed in a particular unit. As with other subject areas, I also offer oral tests to students who have learning challenges that make it difficult for them to take tests.

While every student certainly wants to be on top, a multiage environment provides students with the opportunity to shine in one area even while struggling in another. Each student is seen by his or her peers in a larger way when they spend two or more years working together, so that students who have difficulty with writing are respected for their artistic or speaking abilities, while the most mathematically minded students may need encouragement from their peers in physical education or spelling.

Our district has adopted an interesting assessment tool for fourth graders, the Elementary Science Project Evaluation Tool (ESPET). This hands-on assessment provides additional diagnostic information about students' abilities to make the transition from hands-on experiences to abstract concepts. It shows how well our students are analyzing, interpreting, and generalizing from concrete experiences. We are also given information about students' competence in such skills as recording measurement, weight, and temperature. This sort of feedback allows us to fine-tune our science program. What is more, the students absolutely love taking this test, and they frequently request to take it again the following year when it's time for the next round of fourth graders to be tested.

ADAPTING THE SCIENCE PROGRAM
TO A MULTIAGE CLASSROOM:
A CHALLENGE FOR ALL

We do not divide our students into ability-level groups in science. For this reason, it is important that we offer activities that can be addressed at a variety of levels, providing options for students at both ends of the spectrum. For students working at a more basic level, we offer clear and concise presentations and concrete experiences that translate directly to a conceptual framework. Keener students, however, are provided with opportunities to work at an accelerated pace, explore concepts more deeply, and consciously question their prior models of thinking.

We make accommodations for individual students in a variety of ways:

- Classroom discussions can provide an excellent forum in which spirited and bright students can exchange ideas. I generally begin such a discourse by asking students to clarify a basic conceptual point and then encourage them to question and examine this point more closely. Excitement builds as high-level students challenge one another while the rest of the class picks up their enthusiasm. At the end of the discussion, I return to the basic point, incorporating whatever extensions we have theorized. This format gives all students the opportunity for inclusion in the discussion. In our unit on sound, for example, I began a discussion by asking how high notes differ from low notes in their wave patterns. Each student had already conducted experiments about this distinction, so every student related to this portion of the discussion. I invited a spectrum of students to articulate their observations of high and low notes. I followed by asking, "How would two C notes, an octave apart, vary in wavelength?" This question challenged students to develop theories based on our initial concept about high and low notes that they could subsequently test. Inserting this "what-if" aspect into discussions is exciting to students, and it is educationally valuable so long as students are obliged to give a clear rationale for their theories that is based on prior knowledge and experiences.

- Another means of adding challenge to the science curriculum for high-level students is through classroom contracts, discussed in depth earlier. This system allows me to adapt my expectations according to the needs and abilities of individual students. Although the entire class is given a science assignment each week, I may request that certain students carry out additional experiments or write-ups, while others may be supported through a more abbreviated approach to the lab work.

- Lab reports are a means by which students can respond to science projects according to their levels of understanding. In each lab report, students are asked to respond to particular questions resulting from the lab work. Questions generally deal with observations and hypotheses based on previous experiments. As in the case of math problem-solving write-ups, clear and concise reports that make effective use of visual aids such as charts, graphs, and diagrams are promoted. Stronger students quickly catch on to this "less is more" approach while developing solid skills in scientific writing. Likewise, the teacher can challenge or reinforce students through comments made in their science journals. An individual can be asked to clarify an interesting hypothesis, or it can be suggested that a chart is potentially misleading. This sort of feedback sparks scientific dialogues.

- Independent projects provide a fine opportunity for students to work at their ability level. Most of our science units include a culminating independent project. While the entire class works with the same assessment criteria, I make it clear that my standards will vary according to the ability levels of individual students.

- When I need to prepare for a series of science labs or introduce a new technological skill, I sometimes ask a strong (or less strong) student to assist me during a break or after school. This gives me the opportunity to offer individual students something extra.

BENEFITS OF A MULTIAGE
SCIENCE CLASSROOM

While there are challenges in presenting science skills and concepts to a broad spectrum of students, there are also benefits. As the class moves through a series of concepts, they can be cross-referenced and built upon over a multiyear span. This opportunity to reinforce skills within a broader time frame is invaluable. Last year's unit on Newton's laws informs this year's exploration of structure, which translates further to next year's study of the human body.

In addition to building on science concepts, a multiyear science program encourages an understanding of the scientific process. Over the course of two or more years, students observe, question, hypothesize, design investigations, gather and analyze data, and draw and communicate conclusions. A multiyear plan allows for references to a broader spectrum of prior group experiences than would be possible in a single-year program, thus providing students with more opportunities to see patterns and make connections.

On an individual level, class scientists emerge who become models for other students, whom they inspire and assist. These roles, of course, change from year to year as students come and go and new students grow into leadership roles. A while back, one of my sixth graders told me she had been waiting for two years to enter a two-state essay contest for sixth graders on women in science. Hylda recalled looking up to a previous student who had prepared an extensive research report, and now she was excited about taking on that role herself. She even chose to research the same scientist as her role model. This enthusiasm and depth of interest came across clearly in Hylda's essay. The momentum of her energy carried into the following year, when a subsequent group of students entered the contest, one of whom received an honorable mention for her essay.

Older students love telling younger ones what will come next, and even though we don't tend to repeat units in the same way, there is always a sense of anticipation. While studying electricity, students reminisced back to concepts and experiences from our rocketry unit over a year prior to that time. During our architecture unit, students recalled hearing from previous classmates about structures they had built several years ago.

When I speak with my former students who are now in junior high and high school, they frequently recall academic projects from their intermediate years in rich detail and with great enthusiasm. I believe this is a function of the amount of time they spent in our classroom, contributing to and prospering from the community of learners within. This excitement about learning, paired with a reflective approach, is among the most valuable gifts we can offer our students. In offering this, we are helping prepare our students as conscious and capable citizens in an increasingly scientific and technological world.

7

MULTIAGE MATH

It is the first week of school. I stand in front of the room and pose the following challenge to my grades 4/5/6 class: "If everyone in this room shook hands with everyone else, how many handshakes would there be?" First, we all get up and try to shake and count one another's hands. Everyone realizes we need a better system. "How can we figure this out in a more organized way?" I ask.

"Let's all line up in front of the room, and one person goes at a time," Matt, a fourth grader, proposes.

"Should we include the whole class?" I wonder.

"Let's try it out with just a few students at first, then add more gradually, to see if we can find a pattern," Aurora, a sixth grader, responds.

We see right away that no one shakes their own hand, so the very first person shakes one less hand than the total number of people in the group. We discover that as each successive person takes a turn, there is one less hand to shake, because each already shook hands with the folks who went before. In other words, for three people, there would be 2 + 1 + 0, or three, handshakes. For four people, there would be 3 + 2 + 1 + 0, or six, handshakes. By the time we're up to seven students, everyone in the room has discovered how the pattern works. The students take out their calculators and get to work, checking their totals with one another. Pretty soon we have a consistent answer to the original challenge.

Later in the week, we create this pattern geometrically, using tiles. Some students notice that two step-tile patterns can be fit together like puzzle pieces to form a rectangle. I ask how this pattern might be used to solve the original handshake problem more efficiently. Several precocious students compete with one another to articulate that half of a particular rectangle is the solution.

"How is the size of this rectangle determined?" I question.

A group of interested students works with me to describe the pattern in an algebraic formula:

$$\# \text{ handshakes for } n \text{ people} = 1/2(n) \times (n - 1)$$

They are quite excited about reaching this next level of abstraction. Others have already begun to describe and interpret their solution to the problem in a write-up, including geometric and numerical visuals.

Our class refers to this geometrical/numerical pattern in subsequent problems for the rest of the year, and returning students carry it into the following school year. We call it the "handshake problem pattern." It is a pattern that is compared to other patterns that emerge from other mathematical explorations.

Students are working in small groups on ability-level math assignments. One group of students sits with me around a box of fraction circles. I ask them to show me one-half. "Now, can you give me one-fourth of this one-half?" I request.

After some discussion, a student suggests that the half needs to be divided into four sections, which they all do. Another student in the group announces that one of these four sections equals one-eighth.

"When we work with fractions, the word 'of' implies multiplication," I explain. "So when a problem reads 'one-fourth *times* one-half,' you can think of it as 'one-fourth *of* one-half.'"

After completing a few more increasingly challenging examples with my guidance, I give the group some problems to work on independently. A lively discussion ensues as they unravel each problem together. The next day we use the materials to learn about multiplication with mixed numbers.

Once the concrete process becomes clear, we learn how to multiply fractions on paper, starting with problems that we have completed concretely. As we move into abstract work, we refer back to the concrete model. Occasionally, I ask the students, working individually this time, to represent a fraction problem with a diagram that represents the concrete model we used previously. This helps me determine whether or not a student has internalized an effective mental model.

Students file into the room and open their math books to a page explaining how to convert fractions to decimals. "The fraction three-fourths can also be read 'three divided by four,'" I begin. "What is the answer you get for that division problem on your calculators?"

When the students come up with .75, I ask them to tell me how much three-quarters of a dollar is worth. They all know that the answer is seventy-five cents.

"I'm confused," one student responds, brow furrowed in frustration.

"Sometimes it helps to think in terms of money when learning to compare fractions to decimals, since we are accustomed to speaking of money in both ways," I suggest. "Seventy-five cents is seventy-five one-hundredths of a dollar, or three-quarters of a dollar."

"Oh! I get what you're talking about now," Stevie exclaims, with a sigh of satisfaction. "Can I do the next one?"

After offering Stevie and some others an opportunity to affirm their understanding through several simple examples, we arrive at a new case. "Let's see what happens when we convert one-third to a decimal."

"It's point three three three three three three three three . . . ," Sheala recites.

We learn to use the repeat sign, and we quickly review rounding decimals. Then students complete some problems on their own, as I walk around the room to make sure that everyone is on track.

STRANDS IN THE MATH PROGRAM

The above examples represent three components of our math program. The first example shows a problem-solving activity carried out with the whole class. The second example is a concept lesson, showing how I might introduce the concept of multiplication with fractions. The third example shows a traditional skill lesson. Each of these components is important in helping students form a rich and practical understanding of the mathematical world.

PROBLEM SOLVING IN THE MULTIAGE CLASSROOM

Only the first example is carried out in a mixed ability-level setting. Well-designed challenges like the handshake problem can be solved by students working at a variety of skill and concept levels. It is when students complete write-ups, similar to lab reports, that they reveal their various levels of insight and ability. For the handshake problem, one student might simply calculate the answer using the addition pattern discovered by the class. A second child might notice a relationship among the progressive sums in the sequence, discovering that each time a person is added, the sum increases by the total number of people minus one. In exploring tile patterns, a couple of mathematically minded students noticed that two sets of steps fit together to form a rectangle measuring $n(n-1)$. With just a bit of prompting, several students came up with a formula for finding the solution for total handshakes given any number of people. Those who understood this formula were able to incorporate it into their write-up.

A multiage classroom is an ideal setting for this sort of problem-solving challenge. Students frequently work in pairs on problems that involve hands-on materials. They discuss their observations and theories, and when they are still baffled, they turn to other students in the class. Students who have been in the classroom for a year or two have more experience with these sorts of challenges, and they can nudge the more receptive and capable younger students along.

Assessing Problem-Solving Activities

Individual accountability for understanding a solution occurs when students submit write-ups. These are evaluated according to problem-solving and communication criteria established by the Vermont Math Portfolio and incorporated into a scoring rubric used by students and teachers. The criteria are summarized briefly here:

Problem Solving Criteria:

Approach and Reasoning: How effective and efficient is student's approach?
Connections: Does student make a mathematical connection or observation about the solution?
Solution: Is the solution correct and supported with work?

Communication Criteria:

Mathematical Language and Symbols (terms, vocabulary, symbolic notation): How appropriate and sophisticated are they for student's stage of development?

Mathematical Representations (graphs, plots, charts, tables, models, diagrams):
Are they appropriate, accurate, and sophisticated (for example, cross-referenced)?
Documentation: How clear and complete is the evidence?

We have used this assessment tool with all of our multiage classes since it was first introduced in Vermont in the early 1990s. Initially, I took a huge amount of time each year to introduce the criteria to our class. Now we discuss them in the context of write-ups for particular problems, and the older students provide helpful comments and support for new students. Frequently, students score their own or one another's write-ups. The feedback provided by scores for individual criteria, as opposed to an overall score, helps students understand more specifically what they've accomplished and where they need to stretch a bit more. Through self-assessing and conferencing with peers, students come to see that they can revise and improve a problem-solving write-up just as they might revise another piece of writing.

MATH PROBLEMS
ACROSS THE CURRICULUM

When the Vermont Math Portfolio was first introduced, teachers scrambled to find good problems that would address the assessment criteria. Some of us soon felt that we were introducing problems completely out of context with the rest of our studies, further fragmenting an expanding curriculum. Our first attempts to integrate were superficial, simply changing the incidental characters in a problem to go with a unit theme. Now we seek and develop rich problems that connect with either current math concepts or broader unit themes. Here are a handful of successful problems I have created or adapted through the years:

Three-Layer Corn Bread Challenge (earth science)
This recipe from *The Tassajara Bread Book* is an old favorite of mine. It also has something to do with geology. The Earth has layers, and so does this corn bread. Your challenge is to determine why the corn bread separates into layers and what this has to do with the Earth's layers.

Here's the recipe:

1 c cornmeal (coarse ground works best)
1/2 c whole wheat flour
1/2 c unbleached white flour
2 tsp baking powder
1/2 tsp salt
1 egg
1/4 c honey or molasses
1/4 c oil
3 c milk or buttermilk

Combine dry ingredients. Combine wet ingredients. Mix together. Mixture will be quite watery. Pour into greased pan. Bake 50 minutes at 350 degrees or until top is springy when gently touched. Enjoy!

Family Size at Lincoln Community School (demographics)
The average-size family in the town of Lincoln is 3.07 people. How does that compare with the typical-size family at Lincoln Community School? Explain how you arrived at your conclusion and what it means.

[NOTE: Surveys are a wonderful way to combine math and social studies. Several years ago, I worked with a health educator to develop an entire unit of study based on the nature of time young people spend alone at home. The unit was aptly called "Home Alone" and involved on-line communication between classrooms in several schools.]

Paper Foundation (physics of structure)

Problem: Using only this one sheet of paper and white glue, construct a foundation that will support as much weight as possible.

Limitations: Time limit for construction is one hour. Foundation must be 10 cm tall (plus or minus 5 mm). Foundation will be allowed to dry 23 hours. You will have two trials this week. Try to improve on your first result.

Evaluation: Explain why the strongest foundation works the best. Analyze the quality of your result.

Breath Holding (human body)

What is the typical amount of time a person in our class can hold her or his breath? Use two types of graphs to draw your conclusion.

Diet and Exercise (nutrition and exercise physiology)

Create a menu. Determine how much exercise <u>you</u> would have to do to burn off that yummy meal. (Consider that your body burns a certain number of calories even when you are sitting still.) What have you learned about diet and exercise?

MATH/SCIENCE INTEGRATION

I enjoy designing integrated units of study that include strong mathematical components. Science topics in particular provide fertile ground in which students can learn to apply mathematics skills and concepts.

The Rocket Car Challenge, described in chapter 2, is an example of an integrated math/science design task from our cross-curricular unit on space. While this activity may seem at first like an interesting science lesson, it also supports many learning goals in math. Students applied the R(average) $= D/T$ formula to determine the rate of speed of their cars. They also applied measurement skills, interpreted statistical data, and articulated mechanical and mathematical relationships. While these math skills and concepts were addressed in isolation during our daily math lessons, the Rocket Car Challenge allowed students to begin applying and integrating their learning in a more real-world context.

The primary math goal of the Rocket Car Challenge was to promote the problem-solving portion of the *National Council of Teachers of Mathematics [NCTM] Standards* and our related district and state standards. Student understanding of mathematical content was placed in this context. Diagrams and models were used to explore and express mathematical ideas (mathematics as communication). Data was analyzed by observing the patterns and relationships that emerged with each successive trial run (mathematics as reasoning). Students linked concepts that they learned in class with the physical experience of creating a successful rocket car, thus connecting math to a broader picture of how the world works (mathematical connections). They began to speak in mathematical language to discuss this unfolding view of the world and to describe solutions to the problems they were confronting (mathematics as problem solving and communication).

The Rocket Car Challenge included multiple layers of complexity. Many decisions had to be made in designing and revising the car to meet the desired goal. While the class gathered and shared a common body of data, each student needed to question and determine the value and meaning of their data in connection with their understanding of the original challenge.

To support these connections, I facilitated small- and large-group sharing and questioning of emerging ideas after students had completed the task but before they submitted their portfolio write-ups. There was also much independent discussion among class members throughout and even after completion of the task. This type of opportunity for guided reflection on complex concepts promotes student understanding at a deeper level than would otherwise be obtained. The more accomplished and more articulate students share, clarify, and build on their insights. Those with less to offer gather insights they may have missed on their own, or they discover ways to express what they have already experienced themselves.

This challenge provided options for students at many levels. Through their concrete experiences, students with less ability reached understanding at a basic level (discovering that a lighter vehicle works better), while more sophisticated students analyzed the problem from an integrated systems perspective (incorporating such factors as aerodynamic design, symmetrical proportions, friction, and distribution of weight). Nonetheless, all students reached some measure of success, even if this meant that they discovered why their vehicle didn't work as they hoped it would.

Assessing the Rocket Car Challenge: An Integrated Model

As stated above, individual write-ups of solutions allow me to assess each student's level of understanding. Because my students are well acquainted with the mathematical problem-solving criteria in our holistic scoring guide, we can readily apply them to math/science challenges. Even though we discussed the Rocket Car Challenge as a group, individual write-ups varied considerably. One student included a graph of trial runs showing how the outcome changed in response to certain adjustments. Another student focused on class data, graphing the speed of each car against its balloon circumference. Students were urged to present solutions that cross-referenced data from several different charts and graphs.

Space: Integrated Unit Overview

The Rocket Car Challenge is representative of the mathematical learning experiences that occurred in our integrated unit on space. Parents received a unit overview and two outlines, one detailing social studies and language arts learning goals and another sharing math and science learning goals. The math/science outline read as follows:

MATH/SCIENCE TOPICS ADDRESSED IN SPACE UNIT

Topic	Science Concepts	Math Concepts
Rocketry	Newton's laws of motion friction & gravity air pressure aerodynamics	apply formula: $R(average) = D/T$ measurement rounding & estimation read & create charts graphing & statistics determine altitude using right triangles straight & curved lines
Space Travel	gravity & microgravity	mass vs. weight calculation relationship between weight & gravity
Theories in Astronomy	big bang & nebula theories why planets are round	astronomical numbers timelines & pie graphs
Solar System Stars & Galaxies	relative size & distance; models connecting time & space light-year	————————————> distance vs. time travel powers of 10

My broad math/science goal for this unit was to engage an energetic group of fifth and sixth graders in problem-solving situations that would expand their understanding of math and science skills and concepts while preparing them for more sophisticated academic work.

My expectation was that each learner in our 5/6 classroom, including myself, would put forth his/her best efforts in addressing the tasks and challenges presented. Before each task, I spent hours designing and building my own models, conducting trial runs and flights, and revising my models as needed. My own experiences, frustrations, and discoveries enhanced my ability to support students in their learning process.

INVOLVING STUDENTS IN LEARNING

Many pathways to learning were offered in this unit on space. The design tasks provided a kinesthetic experience. Discussions, presentations, a guest speaker (a rocket scientist), and cooperative and competitive work addressed interpersonal and linguistic skills. Individual write-ups involved introspection and linguistic abilities. Students were asked to create and respond to visual information in the form of diagrams, posters, and videotapes. Technological skills were applied through image processing and computer simulations. Students were also asked to create and respond to MIDI music interpretations of the planets.

The study of rocketry featured several engaging design tasks, such as the Rocket Car Challenge mentioned above. For the "Bottle Rocket Challenge," students created simple rockets from plastic bottles fitted with tire valves. The bottles were pressurized (according to safety standards) with a gauged bicycle pump and blasted off on our school launchpad. A small measure of water could be added to the bottle to create additional thrust. Rocket altitude was measured using an elementary clinometer—based on triangulation and constructed by each student—that was gauged to provide an accurate reading from a distance of thirty meters. After gathering, graphing, and analyzing data, students determined the features of an ideal bottle rocket, incorporating the variables of rocket size and shape and water volume.

Our study of astronomy provided additional opportunities to apply mathematical understanding. To reinforce the concepts of relative size and distance, we created two scaled-down models of the solar system. First, each student charted planetary sizes and distances from the sun on two scales. Next, student pairs each created a papier-mâché model of one planet on the larger scale. Smaller scale models were drawn on posters and used to take a walk through the solar system. Students positioned themselves, with their posters, alongside the quiet road passing by our school at their relative distances apart from one another. This involved students calculating their average pace and then determining how many paces they each needed to walk to reach their relative distance. (Pluto didn't quite make it to its place in the system.) In addition to reinforcing and applying math skills, this activity created a vivid impression of the vast amount of empty space in our solar system.

There were also more abstract tasks in our study of astronomy. Students calculated their weights on each planet and determined the amount of time it would take to travel to a particular planet given various modes of transportation. A couple of students made a game of estimating the time it would take them to reach a given destination in our solar system, traveling at a given speed or determining what rate of speed would take them to each planet within an average life span. Students enjoyed imagining the time factor involved in traveling to a distant planet, and while imagining, they were reinforcing their skills in estimation, computation, and numeration.

Video and computer technologies supported our unit as well. Bill Nye's video did a great job of modeling distances in our solar system. In considering the location of distant galaxies, the students' understanding of vast numbers was supported through the classic video *Powers of Ten*. Image-processing software was introduced to several high-level math students who determined proportional amounts of the moon illuminated in each successive lunar phase. Using simulation software, students competed with one another at spatial games on distant planets, making adjustments for their various gravitational fields.

MEETING THE NEEDS OF A VARIETY OF STUDENTS

A multiage classroom always includes a broad spectrum of learners. The group of students in our room the year we carried out the space unit we've been discussing included both exceptionally high-level students and those with large conceptual gaps. There were also several very active students who had difficulty staying focused. I designed our unit to meet the needs of this latter group in particular and to provide challenge as well as satisfaction to all of my students.

Hands-on activities provide opportunities for many kinds of learners. As depicted in the narrative on the Rocket Car Challenge, I find it works best to present tasks in a clear and efficient manner and quickly let students get to work. Once they are actively engaged, I am free to circulate about the room, providing support and assistance as needed, interacting with individual students to push their levels of questioning and comprehension, and observing the interactions among students. When I notice a number of students overlooking a key point, I bring that point to the attention of the larger group, often by raising pertinent questions for students to answer. Journals and portfolio write-ups also allow me to determine student levels of understanding, and I can then frame subsequent lessons accordingly.

I lobby for long time blocks in our classroom schedule so that students can become fully engaged in their work and see it through to a logical endpoint at their own pace. This atmosphere of independence within guidelines allows students to develop a sense of ownership of their work while allowing me to adjust assignments for students who need more or less challenge.

When students referred back to the space unit at the end of the school year, they all had personal recollections of it as an enjoyable and challenging learning experience.

ASSESSMENT: MONITORING STUDENT UNDERSTANDING

In the types of math and science units under consideration, students are assessed and reinforced through direct observation and interaction, journal entries and responses, portfolio write-ups and scoring feedback, and traditional tests and reteaching. Assessment and follow-up occur throughout such units.

Through careful observation and questioning, I am able to learn a huge amount about each student. It can be difficult to see the difference between a student who is disoriented and one who is pursuing a unique approach to a mathematical problem. By questioning a student about his/her thinking process, I can usually come to a conclusion. I might, for example, ask two students why they have chosen to place larger wheels on the back of their rocket car, or I might challenge them to predict what would change if they replaced all four wheels with the largest variety, or the smallest.

Journal entries are another window into a student's thinking. While some students are quite efficient in their explanations, getting right to the key concepts, others dance around the point, hinting that they aren't clear. There are also perceptive students who have difficulty expressing ideas verbally. I create a dialogue with all of my students in their journals, questioning their thinking or asking them to back up their conclusions with data or take them a step further.

Portfolio write-ups allow me to see if a student is able to integrate skills and concepts. I may be surprised at the high level of conceptual understanding of a student who does not say much in class and who may even have difficulty at the skill level. Alternatively, sometimes students with solid skills may need support in making mathematical connections. Students conference with me or a peer on a draft of their write-up. This encourages reflection, a deeper understanding of the criteria, and meaningful mathematical communication. In response, students generally revise their work before submitting it to me. The final piece results in a portfolio score that students record on their portfolio charts. In this way, students and I become aware of patterns in their problem-solving abilities.

Traditional tests provide information about students' learning in regard to key terms, skills, concepts, and facts. (I sometimes add an open-ended problem-solving challenge to an otherwise objective test.) At the end of the space unit, for instance, every student took the same math/science test, though I gave the test orally to one student who had difficulty with reading and writing. Several students took a retest after they had put in some additional study and review time. In the end, all students performed quite well by the same measure.

MATH SKILLS AND CONCEPTS

The skill and concept lessons described at the beginning of this chapter occur in ability-level math groups. Because math concepts and skills are developed in a sequence that moves toward increasing levels of complexity and abstraction, we divide our students into ability-level groups for this portion of the math program. Students who are considerably below grade level are placed with a younger group of students and receive additional support as needed in or out of math class time. More skilled students work with an older group and are frequently given additional challenges. Students sometimes move from one group to another when we observe their need for more support or challenge in math. Our principal, who has a strong background in math and science, offers a program for above-level sixth graders. I currently teach the sixth-grade-level math group, though it is a multiage group. Over the past several years, our entire school has adopted *Everyday Math*, a curriculum that uses a series of integrated activities designed to deepen students' understanding of mathematical concepts and their relationship to other subject areas and the world outside school. This program, closely aligned with the *NCTM Standards*, paves the way for more sophisticated work in mathematics. I adapt the program to the needs of our group, supplementing it with activities such as the fraction circles presentation described earlier.

SCHEDULING MATH GROUPS

Students currently meet in ability-level groups throughout the school for math instruction. With the adoption of *Everyday Math*, this time period was increased from forty minutes to a full hour. To minimize the impact of the hour-long math block on our day, the upper grades conduct it first thing each morning after attendance.

THE EFFECTIVENESS
OF OUR MATH PROGRAM

The current model for our math program is one that has evolved over the past eight years, and it seems to be serving the needs of our students quite well. Because we have created a personalized program with high goals, many of our special needs students test on grade level by the time they complete sixth grade. Our former students report feeling well prepared for subsequent math work in seventh grade, and their teachers concur with this report. The biggest challenge we've had is that our highest-level students do not always feel challenged when they leave our program.

In prior years, we held math groups in our home-base classrooms in much the same fashion as reading groups. Students worked independently in their ability-level math text, sometimes with the assistance of a classroom aide or community volunteer, while I instructed one of the ability-level groups. Though we had Title I support in the classroom for our needier students, I noted that even many on-level students felt they were not receiving the assistance they needed, particularly as our classes grew in size. And even though I provided them with supplemental assignments, advanced students were not receiving the close guidance needed to inspire them to stretch toward more challenging goals.

Early on we saw the value of a separate math lab for our more needy students. It lowered the number of students in the classroom and allowed both groups of students to work in a focused setting. This was our first step in the transition. Next, we decided to try the math lab model with our entire school. Each teacher assumed responsibility for working with a particular math level. Our principal came on board to offer an above-level program for sixth graders in need of added challenge. (This provided the wonderful side benefit of involving our principal directly in the teaching process.)

Students were universally pleased when we switched to our present model. We now place students at the level of their ability and move them as they show the need. Unless their program calls for an individual aide, special needs students are now placed in the group that best suits them. Mathematical problem solving and integrated math activities continue outside the domain of math groups, maintaining the benefit of multilevel exchanges among students. At the same time, students receive enough direct instruction to keep them motivated, challenged, and progressing.

A PERSONAL PHILOSOPHY

I grew up in a home where math and science were common topics for discussion. Both of my parents were engineers who were fascinated with the beauty and intelligence of the physical world. They helped me enjoy the mathematical relationships around me—in snowflakes and minerals, in bridges and buildings, in rhythmic waves and layered mountains and distant planets.

Later, as a young adult, I studied Maria Montessori's educational pedagogy. I was inspired by her approach to mathematics instruction. She emphasized the use of a sequence of concrete materials wisely designed to move the student toward increasing levels of abstraction. These materials were dovetailed with presentations rich in drama yet grounded in the real world. In this way, Montessori, educated as a scientist, paired the student's vivid imagination with concrete experiences to form an accurate yet awe-filled view of the mathematical world.

I strive to present math with the same sense of wonder and meaning that guided and inspired me in my own learning path.

8

HOME, ARCHITECTURE, AND STRUCTURE: AN INTEGRATED UNIT

Our 5/6 classroom is packed with people and projects. The exhibits cover most of the available space on walls, tables, and the floor area, spilling out even into the hallway. Students usher their parents through the maze of materials.

On one side of the horseshoe of tables is a series of shack sculptures, accompanied by brief, typed vignettes portraying their unseen residents. For example, there is Mr. Bolagh, whose dwelling has a sloping roof decorated with a huge turquoise cone and assorted metal scraps. We learn that he is a retired scientist and an inventor with a great sense of humor.

On the other side of the horseshoe is a collection of carefully constructed architectural models, each accompanied by a graph-paper pre-model and a description of its geographic location and architectural design features. This project is further documented in a video in which each design group has been interviewed about its models. Visitors can view the tape in an adjacent room.

A computer in the corner of the classroom displays a Hyperstudio stack in which students have explained basic structural principles through diagrams, scanned images, text, and sound recordings.

Other displays embellish the walls. A collection of photographs depicts an environmental study of animal homes on the school's nature trail. There are several views of the delightful debris shelters built by groups of students along the trail. Close by is a collection of actual animal homes, including a variety of nests, shells, and hives.

A bulletin board exhibits student poetry and drawings inspired by student novels about homeless children and families. Visitors can browse through the books arranged on an adjacent table.

A large hallway display shows our historic architecture project, a walking tour of ten historic homes in the center of Lincoln a half mile down the road from our school. This display includes labeled house sketches, photographs, collages, and text. There is also an architectural awareness quiz in which parents are asked to establish the location of photographed details of local homes. A group of parents is having particular difficulty with an ornately carved doorway that they can't quite place. (Its location is the side entranceway of an incongruous building several houses from the General Store.)

After visitors have ample opportunity to view the exhibits, we usher them into the multipurpose room for our presentation. First, there is a student-narrated slide show of the historic house tour. Younger students are extremely nervous, but their older classmates cheer them on. Next, there is short poetry/dance performance, a collage of movement and music accompanied by readings of student poems about homelessness.

At the end of the evening, a parent remarks, "I don't see how you could have gone any further with this unit. You covered every possible base."

We smile appreciatively, knowing also that this unit, once the momentum got going, could have lasted throughout the entire year without running out of fuel. In fact, our class went on to create both a videotape and a Web site presenting our historic homes research.

UNIT OVERVIEW

Our Home, Architecture, and Structure unit examined the physics of structure, the historic architecture of Vermont and of our town in particular, basic architectural design concepts, local animal homes, home-related art forms, and the issue of homelessness. Two teachers shared the planning of this unit, and we benefited from the expertise of two environmental education students at Middlebury College. We were also fortunate in receiving grant funds from three sources to support our work in environmental studies and historic homes. The following pages describe how our unit encompassed all content areas. A few of the many connections made across subject areas are also detailed.

Art

Sounds of activity spill out of the fifth- and sixth-grade classroom: hammers banging, saws tearing, asphalt tiles scraping each other, indecipherable materials rolling and dragging and sliding and clanging. The principal is bent over a table, saw in hand; a parent is supervising the use of several glue guns; and I am attempting to help a student either cut or rip some asphalt tiles. But not many voices are heard, for the students are deeply involved in the process of creating miniature shack sculptures based on the work of sculptor Beverly Buchanan. Each shack will become the home of an unseen resident that its builder imagines along with the dwelling. For example, there is Elmer, who has a rough-and-tumble shack made of unpainted wood and some ripped gray asphalt shingles.

Elmer is an old man who lives in a rundown shack on the side of the hill. He lost his job as a bus boy a long time ago, and his wife left him fifteen years ago. His son went away to college and became a lawyer. Elmer hopes the guy at the door will go away.

Not all shacks are like Elmer's. Selene Mercurio has a striking though tidy place, a square-shaped structure painted in thick clean purple and gold stripes, topped with a delicate transparent dome fashioned from cellophane-coated wire. Selene's story is quite different:

Selene Mercurio is a retired movie actress who lives in Oakland, California. She is extremely rich. She was known as the star of the stage, so when she quit acting she decorated her house with stars. She loves jewelry and painted her house gold and silver. Selene has a knack for cards and especially likes the Queen of Hearts card. She likes it so much that she put it on her door. Once, she went to Paris, but her fans were so pushy and rude that she never, ever traveled again. She has a daughter whose name is Marilyn. She, Marilyn, stays with Selene a lot. One day, they went shopping, and Selene bought 53 clothing articles. She really is a fashionable dresser!

At the end of this day-long project, our room looks like a disaster area, and each student has created a marvelous and unique shack along with a vignette describing the individual who dwells or dwelt there. Some of these shacks were later displayed and admired in the Sourdiffe-Furchgotte Gallery in Shelburne, Vermont, as part of an exhibit on dwellings, the theme of which was actually inspired by our students' work.

For the shack project, we read about and viewed photographs of the inspiring work of Beverly Buchanan. We also discussed how the work of an African American sculptor and writer from the rural South might connect with our own lives in rural Vermont. Buchanan's work provided a framework for finding personal expression in one's own shack and story. Clearly, the resulting work was both unified and uniquely inspired.

In addition, students loved the opportunity to immerse themselves in a project of this duration. Early in the day, many students felt their work was complete. Then they looked around at the available materials and other students' work, and they began to get a second level of inspiration. At the end of the day, most students were still deeply involved in the creative process, and many students devoted their break time over the next several weeks to fine-tuning their shacks.

Even though the accompanying writing pieces were short, there was a wonderful interplay between the concept of the unseen resident and the act of assembling the physical structure. Some students worked collaboratively, either teaming up to build one shack or inventing a relationship between their two unseen residents. Some students reveled in the opportunity to freely create a unique and eccentric individual living a solitary existence of their own choosing. Still other students seemed to use this experience as a time to consider some of the challenges that life can hold: loss, separation, and poverty. Because of the range of possible approaches, this was a perfect project for a multiage classroom, where each child had the opportunity to be highly successful and satisfied with her/his work.

Reading

It is valuable to uncover links with thematic units that provide opportunities for students to consider current issues of social concern. We made such a link with our homes unit when we found a collection of excellent novels that created an awareness of the issue of homelessness, not only in our own time and place, but also in other cultures and time periods.

Below is an annotated bibliography of the novels we read, two as read-aloud books, five as group novels (leveled by difficulty), and several others as extensions for interested readers. Readers at every level were interested in and challenged by the readings. For group novels, I created discussion and journal questions as well as essay topics that involved looking more closely at the issue of homelessness at the conclusion of one or more novels.

My students were deeply engaged by these readings, and in discussions they expressed a deep compassion for the plight of homeless children and families. We contacted a homeless shelter to learn more about the issue of homelessness in our area, and our awareness of the reasons for this situation was broadened. A representative from our school's food shelf spoke to students at an assembly, and students participated in a canned goods drive.

Intermediate-Level Novels on Homes and Homeless

Carlson, Natalie Savage. *The Family under the Bridge.* Scholastic, 1958. (Grades 3–6)
French hobo befriends and helps homeless children and their mother.

Fox, Paula. *Monkey Island.* Orchard, 1991. (Grades 5+)
Boy in Manhattan deserted by both parents and lives on the street.

Hahn, Mary Downing. *December Stillness.* Clarion Books, 1988. (Grades 5+)
Fifteen-year-old girl tries to befriend homeless Vietnam veteran.

Harris, Mark Jonathan. *Come the Morning.* Bradbury, 1989. (Grades 5–9)
Family searches for father in California and becomes homeless.

Holman, Felice. *The Wild Children.* Penguin, 1989. (Grades 5–9)
Powerful story of bands of homeless children in 1920s Russia.

Mathis, Sharon Bell. *Sidewalk Story.* Penguin, 1986. (Grades 2–6)
Depicts a present-day urban family in the process of becoming homeless through the eyes of child living down the street.

Nixon, Joan Lowery. *A Family Apart.* Bantam, 1987. (Grades 5–8)
1850s story about six siblings put up for adoption; first in award-winning series.

Tyler, Anne. *The Way Home.* (Out of print.) (Grades 6+)
Peasant girl in medieval times escapes from her village and the plague.

Drama and Dance

Poetry can sometimes reveal the insight and sensitivity of students who are less than fluent writers. Our student poems depicting homeless characters from students' readings were so moving that we decided to use them as the basis for a dance presentation. The words were accompanied, in some cases, by recordings of jazz saxophone or improvisational piano music. Student groups began by pantomiming the words of a poem, gradually abstracting the movements to capture the feeling and shape of the message. The resulting presentation, a component of our homes display held shortly before the winter holidays, had a powerful impact on both adult and child viewers. (One of the student poems is printed in chapter 4.) This project created an opportunity for the more kinesthetically expressive students to shine, and it also allowed students to develop their skills in creative collaboration.

Writing

In addition to the reading-related writing discussed above, we compiled and published a written walking tour of ten historic homes in the center of our town of Lincoln, Vermont. This was a challenging collaborative project in which stronger students were counted on to play a leadership role. Sixth graders were carefully paired with younger partners. After each pair of students was assigned to a particular home, we created and distributed a survey for homeowners and gathered records from the town clerk's office, the local and state historical societies, and local history buffs. We spent a number of Friday afternoons walking through town and observing the features of historic homes. Students formed close relationships with each of their respective assigned homes, becoming intimately aware of its features, history, and owners. All students corresponded with their home's owners, and some were able to arrange personal tours.

When all our data were compiled, we weeded through and organized them into a collection of reports documenting each home through its architectural features and changes, the lore surrounding its past, the lives of its former and present residents, and a few facts describing historic developments in Lincoln during the time period when the house was built. Then came the task of composing an interesting essay about each home, accompanying it with a detailed and labeled architectural drawing of the house. Students also created a series of colorful collages of their respective homes. For the open house, we displayed the artwork, and the students read their reports accompanied by a slide show of the homes. The reports were later published in a booklet, accompanied with timelines of Lincoln, Addison County, and the United States depicting the time period in which the houses were built (the mid-to-late 1800s).

Along the way, this project gathered interest at the local and state levels. Through a grant left to the Lincoln Historic Society, member Steve Harris worked with the students to turn the project into a videotaped tour of the homes. When this was aired in the community at a midwinter festival, other townspeople came forward with more historic information to add to our subsequent publication. We were also able to place our project on a Web site through a state grant that provided us with both equipment and training.

This is an example of a successful multiage project geared to the abilities of upper-level students. While the work was quite sophisticated and at times even tedious for some fifth and sixth graders, the local recognition they received for their accomplishments made them feel it was worthwhile. The booklet and videotape have continued to sell at the Lincoln town clerk's office and historic museum for the past several years, sustaining acknowledgment for our students.

Social Studies

Clearly, our historic walking tour was closely linked with social studies. To support our understanding of local homes, we studied the architectural styles and features of historic homes in Vermont, many of which were built during the same general time frame. We were able to visit a local historic museum that featured a small exhibit on this very topic. The students became adept at identifying styles and elements, and they would spontaneously make a game of it, calling out architectural terms while driving around Vermont on our field trips throughout the school year. Parents reported this same phenomenon during family outings.

Math and Science

"It leaves something to be desired," a student remarks as he examines the detailed Queen Anne porch on the architectural model he's been working on for weeks. This student has set high standards for himself, and he is having a great time doing it.

For the math/science component of our homes unit, students studied the physics of structure. Through a series of design challenges involving straws, sugar cubes, clay, toothpicks, pipe cleaners, glue, paper, and cardboard, students uncovered the principles of such concepts as center of mass, compression and tension, and torque.

Their ultimate task was to create a scale model of their dream home. They could set it in any environment, but they needed to design the building accordingly, even including its orientation to the sun. Students built premodels out of graph paper and then were able to "purchase" a set of raw materials for their actual home, working within a set budget.

Materials included sheets of card printed to resemble bricks, clapboards, shingles, and trim.

In preparation for this final task, the students learned about scale in addition to structure. An architect visited the class and brought students through the process of creating architectural plans, drawings, premodels, and models. The students echoed this process in their own work. A parent who works as a building contractor also worked with the students, showing them the blueprints for our new school playground that was currently under construction and demonstrating the use of a CAD (computer-aided design) program.

Students worked with great focus on their models for several weeks, discussing design features and geographic impact with much animation throughout this time period. When the projects were complete, each set of architects wrote up a description of their home and its setting to accompany the models. The videotaped interviews with students (noted previously) revealed that students had become familiar with many of the factors that come into consideration when designing a home.

The architectural component of our unit also challenged our multiage students, yet they had full control of the level of complexity they would incorporate in their homes. Many students began with highly elaborate plans and then simplified them as they realized what each feature entailed. In some cases, students were encouraged to stay the course and work through the frustrations to a satisfying endpoint, just as the student above was doing with his Queen Anne porch.

Technology

The possibilities for incorporating technology into a unit such as this are endless. We focused on several aspects: using the word processor to create our class publication, creating a multimedia stack on the principles of structure, and designing a Web page to display our historic homes project, in that order. This sequence of projects moved the students from basic computer concepts to more sophisticated ones. Returning students helped the newer students or those with less technological expertise.

To support the first assignment, students used a typing program to improve their keyboarding skills. I also created an on-screen worksheet in which students were asked to alter a page by changing font size and styles, margins, and placement of text through the cut, copy, and paste functions. Although we used a consistent font for the text of our booklet, each student group designed the heading of its report.

For their Hyperstudio stack, students designed cards according to their levels of expertise. Some worked with simple text and graphics layouts, while others imported and manipulated graphics or scanned a series of images onto their cards. The most adept students oversaw the project, creating the home page and making sure all of the buttons worked appropriately.

Creating the Web site was our ultimate technology project of the year. Because of the level of skill involved, it was less directly satisfying than creating a multimedia stack. Nevertheless, the students felt a high level of accomplishment once the project was completed very close to the end of the year. (Actually, we adults needed to revise some images afterward, as explained below.)

We managed this project through the use of student tutors. After I was somewhat familiar with our Web-composing software (we used Adobe® PageMill®), I worked with our keenest student technologist to create a home page. He went on to create his page and then dubbed himself "Web Master." At this point, I assigned him to a couple of other students who I knew would catch on quickly so that we would have a base of student teachers. From here, the rest of the students ventured through the process.

I am cautiously optimistic about using students as technology educators. I check in with them frequently and set clear limits on their authority to make adjustments on the computer, especially where the system is involved. The technologists are generally innovative problem solvers, but there can be other problems along the way. For example, our resident Web Master figured out an extremely clever way to solve the issue of creating wonderfully clear images on our Web pages. The only problem was that it would take about five minutes to download some of them. For this reason, my job-share partner and I spent a full day in June revising the images to make them less memory intensive. Still, the assistance of our Web Master allowed all students to complete their own drafted pages during school hours.

Environmental Education

The environmental portion of our unit was directly supported by the Watershed Partnership, a grant provided through Middlebury College, the Orion Society, and the Geraldine R. Dodge Foundation. For this component, our class studied animal homes, animal architecture, and the use of native materials in human dwellings.

There was a significant multiage benefit with the environmental component of our unit. This was our second round in a two-year grant; half our students had participated during the previous year in a botany project that also made use of the nature trail on our school grounds. These students came into the project with related knowledge that enriched their personal learning as well as the discussions and experiences among the whole group.

Two Middlebury College student interns—Wendy and Jess—worked with half the students for two afternoons each week. Under their guidance, students made sound maps of the trail, searched for amphibians and land animals, and collected and observed water animals in the river. They simulated a bird's experience by taping their fingers together before attempting to build nests of twigs, pine needles, and leaves. They moved a step beyond reality, creating detailed drawings of imaginary insects, complete with descriptions of each creature's habitat and food sources.

After becoming familiar with the habitats along our nature trail, each student chose one native animal to research and sketch. These drawings, along with their stories, became the basis for a winter advent calendar in which animals and stories were unfolded one by one from inside their nests, burrows, and dens in a student-painted mural.

Periodically, we held sessions with the full group. On one such occasion, the class viewed the video *Animal Architecture*. In our subsequent discussion about principles of structure, students drew links between animal and human architecture. Later, students composed poems about home building written from the point of view of the animal. One sixth grader wrote "Horse Fluff Bird's Nest" for this exercise, a poem based on an experience while grooming her horse. This poem resulted in a collaborative poetry/dance piece presented with the homeless pieces at the open house for our homes and architecture unit.

Horse Fluff Bird's Nest

As I fly over the land
I sing my beautiful song
I see a young girl brushing and grooming a horse

She takes a bit of fluff
And holds it in her hand
The wind grabs it from her hand, pulling it to the sky
I swoop down and grab it
Then fly to a nearby tree
I drop the fluff on a branch
Then fly down to the earth
And pull 30 strands of long golden color grass
Then I fly back to the tree
I take the fluff and grass
And start to build my cup-shaped nest
When I am done
I sit and lay my eggs
Five beautiful bluish speckled eggs
When they hatch
My husband will find food
And we both shall care for our young

—Hylda Rood

Another class session, and a highlight of the unit, was spent constructing debris huts along our nature trail. Students read through a collection of books on Native American homes built from native materials, then used these ideas to design a plan for their own shelters. Two crisp afternoons were spent constructing shelters from fallen twigs and branches and leaves. The first day was spent creating the "bones" of the structure, while the second session was used to cover them with some form of "skin". A number of students designed huts under or alongside the protection of low-hanging or thick trees, while others fashioned sturdy freestanding designs.

This activity struck a deep chord in all of the students. Their resulting structures were playful, practical, and unique. There were tepee and dome-shaped huts, longhouses and lean-tos; some were big enough for just a tiny creature, while others could easily shelter two or three students. We returned to these huts throughout the changing seasons of our school year, repeatedly finding many of them intact. Crawling inside on a day in February, students noticed how the interiors provided insulation. As we approached, someone saw a mouse scurry out of a shelter one chilly afternoon.

On our last day of school in June, half a year after the completion of our homes unit, wildflowers finally speckled the fields, and the river glistened. As a closing ritual, we took a walk along our nature trail. Many shelters remained standing. Students rushed up to examine their own, climbing inside and peering whimsically out, reclaiming the little dwellings they had created months ago. As I walked past a sturdy tepee-shaped hut, Zeb popped his head out and waved at me. It was clear from these exhibits of enthusiasm that the learning experiences we planned for our students had left a mark and that the young people crawling out of the fanciful forts along our nature trail will remember these moments as significant. Perhaps, at the very least, these images will remain with them to underscore their sense of belonging to the wonderful community that is their home.

Walking back to the classroom, students wondered if our huts would last into next fall. Like our school year, some parts would sift away while the places that were built securely would remain, providing the recesses and ledges in which to place future experiences.

ASSESSMENT

Student work in this unit was assessed through all the means discussed in previous chapters: math and writing portfolio criteria, collaboratively designed scoring rubrics, journal entries, anecdotal observation, and traditional tests. We kept parents informed about the unit and their child's work through notes, formal reporting, and the open house. The open house allowed parents to view their child's work beside the work of many other students, and teachers were present to enrich their observations. Students also assessed their own work in this unit through the following form.

✿✿

Self-Assessment Sheet for 5/6 Homes Unit
Lincoln Community School

Name:

Key: **E** = Exceptionally well
      F = Fairly well
      S = Somewhat well
      N = Needed improvement

Historic House Project

_____ I did a thorough job on my research.

_____ I used all the important information in my report.

_____ My partner and I shared the work and collaborated well. (Explain as needed.)

What I did especially well on this project:

What I would change or add next time:

Shack Sculptures and Stories

_____ My shack creates the feeling of an unseen resident.

_____ My story is compatible with my shack.

What I did especially well on this project:

What I would change or add next time:

Homeless Poetry

_____ My poem effectively captures the feeling of homelessness.

_____ I used interesting words, word patterns, and/or figures of speech.

What I did especially well on this project:

What I would change or add next time:

Homeless Dance/Poetry Presentation

_____ Our dance piece worked well with our poem.

_____ Our dance piece made good use of space.

_____ Our dance piece had a clear high point.

_____ Our dance piece made good use of timing.

_____ The members of our team collaborated well.

What I did especially well on this project:

What I would change or add next time:

Homeless Readings

_____ I kept up with readings.

_____ I kept up with questions.

_____ I participated appropriately in discussions.

What I did especially well on this project:

What I would change or add next time:

Homeless Unit (in general)

What I liked best about this unit:

What I would suggest changing or adding next time:

✢✢✢

CLOSING THOUGHTS

As the discussion above shows, a multiage integrated unit can provide rich experiences across the curriculum for a broad spectrum of students. When careful thought and planning goes into articulating goals, gathering resources, and defining learning experiences, the rewards are great for students—and for teachers.

II

THE BENEFITS OF THE MULTIAGE CLASSROOM

9

THE PERSONAL AND SOCIAL BENEFITS OF ELEMENTARY MULTIAGE CLASSROOMS

We don't act like fourth, fifth, and sixth graders. We just act like kids at school, learning. We get to make a lot of choices by ourselves. Mostly everybody gets along. The teachers are the best. What I mean is, they are nice and they trust our opinions.

—Fifth- grade student in 4/5/6 multiage classroom

I interviewed seven teachers with a combined seventy-five years of elementary school teaching experience, of which thirty-nine years had taken place in multiage classrooms that they had designed and operated. What these teachers articulated includes: (1) the defining qualities of multiage classrooms; and (2) from these teachers' perspectives, the personal and social benefits of such classrooms for students, teachers, and parents.

Each teacher felt strongly that a multiage classroom begins with a philosophical commitment by a teacher and requires that teachers—and schools—maintain this commitment over time. "It can't be just a way to solve a numbers problem," Alice Leeds, grades 5/6 multiage classroom teacher at Lincoln Community School in Lincoln, Vermont, explained. "The teacher has to believe in and understand its value. Then you need school leadership and policy to support [the] multiage [approach], so they don't toss it away whenever the numbers shift a bit."

What are the elements of this philosophical commitment? Each of the seven teachers identified the following:

- Multiage classrooms include students with at least a two-year span in chronological age, who would previously have been placed in two different grades.
- Each student remains in the same classroom with the same teacher(s) for at least two school years, often longer.
- The teacher learns to perceive each student not as a member of a grade grouping, but as the individual she/he is, with a multiplicity of qualities and capabilities, not all of which are at the same level of development.

> Pat Minor (grades 2/3 multiage classroom teacher at Beeman Elementary School, New Haven, Vermont): "You have technically more than one grade in the classroom. But once they've walked through the door, I don't think about them as just second graders or third graders. They're kids, and they have varying degrees of abilities and you take them where they are, see what skills they have, and what they need to work on. In this class, we have kids who are from six years old when they walk in to ten years old. Multiage is exactly what these kids are."

- The children learn to perceive one another less and less in terms of grade membership and more and more in terms of specific personal qualities and capabilities. Chronological age becomes less important as a determinant of children's relationships, while developmental age becomes more important.

> Debbie Cross (grades 4/5/6 multiage classroom teacher at Beeman Elementary School, New Haven, Vermont): "In the multiage classroom, there's a place for everybody; everybody fits somewhere. It's okay for a sixth grader, say, to be friends with a fourth grader. They care for each other, and they help each other."

- A multiage classroom generates more profound relationships between teacher and students, among students, and between teacher and parents. Indeed, each of these seven teachers used the metaphor of family to characterize the social qualities of their classrooms.

> Debbie Cross: "It's a family and a community. It's a feeling that you foster and that you look for."

Carol Hasson (grades 4/5 multiage classroom teacher at Robinson School, Starksboro, Vermont): "In a multiage classroom, the students, along with the teacher, take on roles similar to those in a family. The atmosphere is like a family. Comfort and trust are two key characteristics. Dependence, or interdependence, is also really important. Knowing that you will all be together for more than one year allows you to become invested in really getting to know and trust each other. And you are more likely to know personal things about each other. Parents are more likely to share problems that are going on at home. You're just all working together more. That's what I think of as a family: everybody works together."

- The qualities of the multiage classroom encourage the teacher to begin a transformation of her/his pedagogy. In this work, the teacher moves from teaching to an imaginary "middle of the class" to conceiving and structuring learning activities that meet the needs of diverse individuals.

Jodi Lane (grades 1/2 multiage classroom teacher at Robinson School, Starksboro, Vermont): "There are a lot of different levels in a multiage classroom, and you're able to individualize and have kids working at their own level, at their own pace. But you're also able to do a lot of small-group activities, and some whole-group ones, too, that are more open-ended, that meet all those different levels."

John Bourgoin (grades 4/5/6 multiage classroom teacher at Beeman Elementary School, New Haven, Vermont): "Units or activities are planned for participation by the whole group much of the time. But the individual student's work may be more individualized; the expectations will probably vary, depending on the individual's needs."

In conversations I've had not only with these seven multiage teachers, but with several dozen others, each has articulated a very similar perceptual and conceptual shift that is generated by the recognition of the defining element of the multiage classroom: a wider age range. Almost all teachers know that every single-grade classroom contains students with a wide range of developmental levels and that each child embodies her/his own wide range of developmental abilities. Yet the very structure of age grading encourages most teachers to perceive their students as similar and to conceive of teaching as an activity directed toward the whole class.

In contrast, a multiage classroom is obviously different, and this difference encourages teachers to begin a reinvention of their activity. Teachers are freed to perceive students as diverse, both in relation to one another and to their own individual set of qualities and capacities. This perceptual shift leads teachers toward reconceiving the nature of instruction and relationship within their classrooms.

THE BENEFITS OF MULTIAGE CLASSROOMS: FOR STUDENTS

> There's one [fourth-grade] kid in my class; he's very skilled, and he's in most of my groups. He does a lot with me because he's smart for his age, and we always work together because he's fun. . . . If the other younger kids need help with something, I can help them—you know, spelling or figuring out a math problem.
>
> —Sixth-grade student in 4/5/6 multiage classroom

> I think you learn to work with the younger kids and not to feel like you're better than them because you're older. . . . When we mix the classes together, everyone seems to be more friendly to each other than when we were in separate grades. It seemed like you really had to learn to work with all different kids. You had to learn to work with them instead of thinking you're better.
>
> —Sixth-grade student in 4/5/6 multiage classroom

What are the benefits for students of multiage classrooms, from the perspective of these seven experienced teachers?

1. Every teacher perceived an increase in the quality of the relationship between teacher and student, experienced by students as follows: greater knowledge of the student's capacities and needs by the teacher; greater consistency of the teacher's behavior and expectations; greater comfort and security felt in the classroom; and greater mutual caring and concern.

> Pat Minor: "There is the possibility of continuity with teachers. For some children, that is absolutely essential, for them to be comfortable, to feel secure; and nobody, if they're uncomfortable or are not settled, will learn to their best potential. And the kids, when they come in after I've had them for one year, they come back in and they're really on top of it. They

really understand what's expected, and they're ready to work the first day they walk in."

Alice Leeds: "The benefits are, they get to evolve over a three- or two-year period, so they don't have to get to know the teacher again. Once they're integrated with the classroom, they're going to be there awhile, and they can feel comfortable and really settle in. So it builds a certain amount of confidence and continuity."

Carol Hasson: "For students, I think the consistency of having the same teacher for more than one year is the biggest benefit of multiage classrooms. The consistency, knowing the expectations and the routine, allows kids to feel safe, and you see fewer behavior problems and acting out to get attention. Kids who come in labeled as behavior problem kids—usually by the second year, those behaviors are minimized because they're into the routine, they know the expectations, and it's consistent for them. Shy kids tend to become more relaxed and come out of their shells. Followers tend to feel safe to explore being leaders."

2. Each teacher noted that the social climate of a multiage classroom is more positive in a variety of ways. One element of this involves the recognition of diversity by the students and their increased acceptance and even valuing of differences among their peers.

Pat Minor: "I think the kids are also much more accepting of each other. They're not so judgmental because there is a huge range. . . . So they're much more accepting of each other and of what kids do and what they can't do. I think they've come to realize that everybody is not always going to be good at everything, that some kids are really good at this—so-and-so can do this really well, while this other area they really need to work a lot harder in. And they're much more accepting of that. And I think it's much more motivating when they don't feel out of place, put down. And their self-images are much more positive by the end of the year. They're much more eager to go on and to work harder by the end of the year because of how they feel about themselves."

John Bourgoin: "It's almost like there's more opportunity for a greater number of kids to be able to have individual strengths and responsibilities. Whereas, different than in a single-grade situation where things always leveled off, I think there's more flexibility in multiage grouping for a greater number of kids to be able to stretch."

Arnell Paquette (grades 4/5/6 multiage classroom teacher at Beeman Elementary School, New Haven, Vermont): "It's just so safe in the multiage setting for the kids to work on whatever level they need to be on. I think it's rewarding academically for a younger child to be able to work with a sixth grader, but also for a fourth grader who is perhaps really needy to see that, 'Gee, there's a fifth grader doing the same thing or a sixth grader doing the same thing that I'm doing, and it's okay.' I think it's just a safer environment emotionally for kids."

Alice Leeds: "So if they're a slow student or an accelerated student, it's not like, 'Oh, gee, of all the fifth grade, this kid can't do fractions yet, or this kid is way, way ahead.' Where they're at is not so crucial, and it's not such a visible thing because it's a given that they're all over the place in ability levels, so they get to be where they are. Other students, of course, notice, but it doesn't seem to be such a stigma or a big deal."

Another element of the increased positivity in the social environment of the classroom is the reduction of negative norms.

Debbie Cross: "One of the biggest things I see . . . is all that negative role modeling that sixth-grade students demonstrate, especially when our school only goes up to sixth grade, that cockiness, that 'I'm cool' stuff—it was just virtually eliminated the first year [we went to multiage] because they have to be role models. . . . All that preadolescent stuff, twenty-five of them in the classroom at one time. It's awful. And to split them up and have them be role models and to intertwine with other kids, it's a joy."

John Bourgoin: "It's not common to see or hear a child judge another one based on whether they're a good student or not. That's a rarity. . . . They're aware of differences, though, and I think because of that awareness, they are much more inclined to try and remedy the situation, by helping another kid, as opposed to using it against them."

3. Each teacher described the ways in which students of different ages become increasingly interdependent within a multiage setting, because they often teach one another. This peer tutoring and interdependence leads to better learning and enhanced self-esteem.

Alice Leeds: "[Teaching a peer] builds confidence that you really know something. If you really know something well, you can explain it to another child. And they have to know things well enough that they can explain it to someone else. They're constantly in that situation of explaining it to someone else."

Jodi Lane: "Putting kids together with partners allows them to teach something so they can learn it even better, as you have to really know something in order to teach it to another child. They all like to do that for each other, not just the older kids. The younger ones, too."

Debbie Cross: "Kids are more apt to offer help to each other in a multi-age [classroom]. They see somebody working on something and go, 'Oh, I know how to do that; let me show you.' They take it upon themselves."

John Bourgoin: "What's happened as time has gone on is that the younger kids have discovered that they have some things that they could help somebody else with, too. And so there's a constant asking, 'Can so-and-so help me?' and much more of a seeking each other out for assistance, not a direct relying on the teacher all the time. So they begin to see each other as having something to offer in terms of knowledge, as well as social things."

A related outcome to the increase of interdependence, then, is increased independence of children from the teacher as they learn to rely on one another as facilitators of learning.

Alice Leeds: "I see students in my classroom become more willing to take care of questions or problems for themselves as the year or years go on. They ask me less often as the first option and try to figure it out for themselves, either with a peer or alone, first thing. Then, if they're still stuck, they come to me."

4. Every teacher noted that children in a multiage classroom experience a much wider range of group roles than in single-grade experience. Each child has the opportunity to be an "elder," a leader, a role model in the classroom.

Jodi Lane: "For many older kids, being able to be the person who is the role model is extremely important and encourages them to become responsible leaders. I have very few behavior problems this year, none really. And I think that a lot of that comes from being able to be the older kid in charge."

Pat Minor: "[Children in the second year in the class] . . . are really the leaders. If they have been in a class for a year, they take a leadership role, and for some of these kids, this is the first time this has ever happened to them. . . . Also, they become role models for the younger kids and buddies and instructors in a lot of ways, helping the [new] kids to get settled in."

Alice Leeds: "As they get older, they get to become leaders and role models, and they become sort of assistants to the teacher. I don't mean this in a way that it takes away from their own work. I think sometimes parents worry about this, about children taking on responsibilities. I see it as very positive. It builds confidence, and they develop leadership skills and group skills."

Carol Hasson: "I was worried entering this school year because, looking at my fourth graders, I couldn't see any strong leaders emerging among them as they turned into fifth graders. I was concerned about this since I depend on the students I've already had in class to set the stage and become role models for the younger kids. Thankfully, I was pleasantly surprised to see kids who'd been followers take on leadership roles and blossom into strong leaders and role models. I don't think this would have happened for these kids had this not been a multiage classroom."

Many children also experience a role that differs from that of their family birth order.

Carol Hasson: "[The] multiage [setting] gives kids an opportunity to experience roles different from those they have in their family. For instance, a child who is the youngest at home will get a chance to reverse that role and become an older child. She'll get to feel what that's like and have that kind of responsibility. She'll have the opportunities that go along with being an older child, as well as the negative things about being older. And if you're an older child in your family, it's vice versa. Experiencing these different roles can help kids gain a better understanding of themselves and of their relationships with siblings."

5. Each teacher explained that a multiage classroom eases the stress of entering a new classroom for the child and allows the teacher to pay more attention to each new student.

Alice Leeds: "When students enter in, they're not part of a huge group of kids that are all new. Maybe half or two-thirds have already been there and help them adjust. It's not just one teacher getting them ready; they have a lot of students who are helping them adapt. In fact, in our classroom, we have a peer partner program. They all have peer partners, so they don't have to wait every time they have a question on procedure or content or whatever. There's always a student right there who can help them answer a question. . . . And I can get to know each new student much more quickly because there's a manageable number of them."

Several teachers noted that multiage classrooms help children focus on learning just by reducing the number of transitions in their school career.

Debbie Cross: "Another benefit for the kids is the continuity from year to year. One fourth grader was saying how hard fourth grade was because it was such a change. And I said, 'Well, you should talk to Jonathan about fifth grade and how it's different.' And he had already, and Jonathan had said that fifth grade is so much better because you know the teacher, you know what needs to happen. When they go into fifth grade, there's that familiarity and that comfort that they don't have to worry, and therefore, often the academics take over."

6. Several teachers reflected that multiage classrooms can help teachers address the dilemma of failing a student during the elementary years in a way that gets them "out of the box" of two poor choices: failing or social promotion.

Pat Minor: "If kids need an extra year to spend in the class, they can have it. Instead of spending two years, they can spend three years. And there's half of the class that they've been with that they can be with again, and the stigma that has always been associated with repeating or spending extra time in a group isn't there. We've done this with a few kids, and they do better with the extra time. And nobody calls them a failure."

With multiage classrooms, the need to judge each student's readiness for the next grade each and every year is removed. In single-grade classes, a teacher must begin the process of decision in terms of passing or failing a student as soon as January if she/he is to follow the required procedures in many schools. This requirement for deciding each student's fate inevitably clouds the teacher's efforts to connect with and teach children who are at risk of failure. In contrast, multiage teachers know that they have a great expanse of time during which they can focus on a child's learning needs without having to worry about "flunking" the child.

THE BENEFITS OF MULTIAGE CLASSROOMS: FOR TEACHERS

Yeah, if you stay with a teacher for three years, well, she knows what you're good at and what you can do. And it makes you work harder. . . . And when we're the oldest, we can help the fourth graders and be, like, role models. That's how you act and stuff. They take on what you do. Like, if you act good, that's probably what they'll act like, because you set good examples.

[In response to question: Do you remember what the older kids did when you were in fourth grade?]: *I remember some of it. They were always getting their work done and stuff, and acting pretty good and stuff.*

—Sixth-grade student in 4/5/6 multiage classroom

All seven teachers spoke with conviction about the benefits of multiage classrooms for teachers. Obviously, some of the benefits for teachers complement the benefits for students.

1. When asked to rank the order of the benefits of multiage classrooms for teachers, each teacher listed "deeper, more profound relationships with kids" and "greater personal rewards in seeing students' growth and learning" as the most significant rewards. Teachers consistently spoke of these two outcomes in tandem, identifying them as interrelated phenomena.

Alice Leeds: "I think the biggest benefit is that you get to work with the child over two or three years, and when the child comes back, you can pretty much pick up where you left off. You can set very long-term goals for children; you don't have to say, 'By the end of the year, I've got to get them here.' You take a longer and a broader vision with the child, and I think in that way, your goals are not as superficial. You don't just say, 'I've got to get them to know their times tables.' So you think in terms of, 'I'd like to see this child develop more social confidence, I'd like to see this child be willing to take on more leadership or take on more challenge, and I'd like to see them be able to follow through.' You start to see each child more as a person rather than just as somebody you've got to give so many skills to, and you work on things in a broader way. I used to say that you have a second and a third chance, but now I see it as much more than that. You take a look at the person; you develop a relationship with them; you develop a relationship with their family; so you see them in a broader context, not just as a kid who is in your classroom. You develop more compassion; you develop a relationship, because you care. You grow to love the children, and you feel relationship with them. So that, I think, is the big one, that you get to know those kids and work with them and see them progress over a long period of time. And it's always wonderful to witness their growth."

Jodi Lane: "Being able to know right where they are at the beginning of the second year is great. If I were to send kids on after one year, I just wouldn't see their continued growth. And there are some kids who really need that second year to grow. It gives me wonderful feedback when I have kids for two years and they didn't quite get it that first year. But by the end of that second year, wow, look how much they've got. And that's really rewarding for me."

Carol Hasson: "I think you become more invested in a child's education when you teach that child for two years or more. You know the child is going to be with you, and you know that I'm playing a big role in this person's education. And I think you care more because you get to know the child more. Sometimes you might go through a whole year having a child in your class and not ever really get to know her. That child goes on, and you always wonder, 'Did I do enough?' In a multiage [class], you always have that second year to do even more."

John Bourgoin: "I think time is the one issue that is really a big difference as far as being able to have a kid from one year to the next. I've always felt that there are certain children [about whom] I would say, 'This kid's going to get there, but the kid just needs some time.' And I would never see it happen, because they would leave. Whereas now I can say, about a particular kid, 'I'm not going to get too uptight about this kid this year. I know what the kid needs; the kid isn't really ready; the kid needs some time.' I'm not going to get on his or her case right now. I don't need to; it's just going to make them anxious. And then the following year, it's like, 'I knew this kid needed some time. That's all it took.'"

Debbie Cross: "For myself, it's much more rewarding to have a child for more than one year because you see the blossoming. Some of my kids in this class I've had three years, and it's just incredible to look back and see them. One student my colleague had for three years, and he kept him for a fourth year because he needed it. And just to see how that child has grown is really rewarding, much more so than straight grades."

2. Every teacher described the ways in which multiage classrooms minimize the stress of starting a new school year and support productive use of schooltime right from the first week of school.

Pat Minor: "It takes a good two months to settle a new class in: to find out where they're at, to get them to understand the routine and expectations. And for me to get to know where they are, how they work, so I'm comfortable with them. But with a multiage [class], the first week of school, we're rolling. I mean, I never had that before. The first year of multiage [teaching], I was shocked; I was absolutely blown away. I went home saying, 'This is too easy.' It was so much less stressful than it had ever been before. Now when I start the year, I know half the kids already, their strengths and weaknesses. I know what they missed last year and where the holes are. I know where I can go with them. And the [new] kids seem to fit right in."

Carol Hasson: "There's none of that time in the beginning of the year where the teacher has to get to know the students and the students get to know the teacher, and all that's wasted in the process, especially for kids who have a difficult time with transitions and new environments."

Alice Leeds: "One thing is that every year you don't have to integrate a whole new class of kids. You really can integrate the new kids more easily into the room, and the other children help you do that. One girl said a couple of years ago when she became a fifth grader and the new fourth graders came in, she said, 'You know, it's much easier when you come back.' The kids really help get each other going."

Jodi Lane: "At the end of the year, I know exactly where they left off. When they come back in, it's just amazing how much things fly from that point on."

3. Each teacher explained that a key benefit of multiage classrooms is the development of stronger and more productive relationships with the parents of their students.

Carol Hasson: "Kids know that I've gotten a relationship going with their parents, and the communication is much more frequent and more comfortable. So I think that it makes the kid know that both people [teacher and parent] are communicating. I feel like I develop a really intimate relationship with my [students'] parents over the two years, and I think that's really good for kids to know."

Pat Minor: "You really get to know parents because a lot of times, the parents come in with the same set of fears and expectations. You have to get to know the parents in order for them to help their kids and be supportive of the school system and know what we're doing and where we're going. After one year, they get to know me, and so they know how I'm handling their kid. We can work together through problems that their kid has, maybe concerns they have. We have to work together to do this. They get so if they have concerns, they can call me or write me, and I can talk to them, call them and say, 'I really think your child will benefit from summer school this summer to keep [him] going' or 'She really needs to be worked with on this or that behavior. This is what we're working on.' Or maybe there's been some stress in the family for some reason, and we can talk about it, work it through, and help their child."

Alice Leeds: "I really think parents make more of a commitment to their relationship with me as their kid's teacher in a multiage [class] than they did in a straight grade. It's like, well, they know they're stuck with me for a long time, and I'm going to be important to their child, so they're more willing to work at it, to put more effort into things."

Jodi Lane: "I think the relationship that I am able to develop with the parents is incredible. Even parents who tend to be a little hard to get to know—When you have them for two years, you see them double the time that you would see them in one year, and by the end of those two years, you really know them well."

Arnell Paquette: "When you have kids more than one year, you begin to build a relationship with the parents, and it builds. The first year it might be kind of sketchy, but after a year, in the second year and maybe the third year even, it's different. It's not your typical parent–teacher relationship in that it can be more of a partnership because it builds from year to year. I find that to be really easy. It makes it easier to deal with kids because you've got two or three adults working for the kid."

Debbie Cross: "I find them [parents] much easier to approach, and they approach me more often. I get phone calls at home or notes or whatever. I think that there's a comfort for them, too. It isn't formal at all after the first year; it really is quite different."

John Bourgoin: "There used to be a formality to the parent–teacher conferencing or the getting together for whatever before. And now, [with multiage], it's become much more of an open dialogue that you can have with the parent about their child. I find myself being a lot more candid than I used to be."

Debbie Cross: "It's been very interesting in the last year and recently to see more and more requests, because we originally had said that we'll keep the child for two years because we didn't think it might be wise to keep them for three years. And now we're getting more and more requests to keep the child for three years from parents, which is real interesting."

4. Several teachers identified the continuity from year to year that multiage classes create as a significant benefit.

Debbie Cross: "Another benefit for the teachers is the continuity from year to year. You start thinking and planning in cycles of several years, and once you get the hang of it, it seems to make things easier."

Carol Hasson: "Planning instruction is a lot easier in a multiage classroom. You know the kids, their needs, likes and dislikes. You aren't spending all that time trying to figure out what they need, so your units are better. The following year, you know where they've been and where they need to go."

5. Finally, every teacher expressed a philosophical commitment to multiage classrooms and in one way or another noted that such a commitment brought focus and renewed purpose to their professional lives.

John Bourgoin: "I think one of the benefits for me on a personal level has been that I've always felt that this [multiage approach] was what teaching should really be and that this was the natural, if you want to call it that, way to teach; that it was very unnatural to take children from a natural setting like a family and then put them into this building or space and then work under the assumption that because you are a nine-year-old, that means you have this bulk of information that you have to master and learn because Houghton Mifflin, or whoever publishes the textbook, says in the fourth-grade textbook that that's what nine-year-olds need to know. It just went against a lot of my own native instincts about how I felt kids learned and how I felt that I should be teaching them. It's a lot more work in one sense, but in the other sense, it's much more rewarding because I feel that I'm doing what children need for me to do as a teacher."

THE BENEFITS OF MULTIAGE CLASSROOMS: FOR PARENTS

Your parents get to know your teacher after a while. They're not afraid to talk to them and tell them stuff. So, sometimes I don't like it that much, but most of the time it's pretty good, you know, that your parents and the teacher can talk and get along and help you and stuff.

—Sixth-grade student in 4/5/6 multiage classroom

The teachers also saw several clear benefits for parents in the multiage classrooms of their children. These benefits focus on the increase in comfort that parents feel when they can get to know a teacher over more than a year and the greater likelihood that parent and teacher can work together to support a child's growth and learning.

Carol Hasson: "I think some parents are really afraid to come into schools and are intimidated, and they feel a lot more comfortable not having to get to know another person the next year. Both [a colleague] and I had a parent who last year hardly ever came to conferences. She started coming halfway through the year, and then she started to come for the rest of the year. This year she started out the year coming, and I know that wouldn't happen if she'd started out with totally new teachers. I think she would have still felt that intimidation. So I feel like they feel more comfortable with you, and they're used to your routines. All my parents know, as fourth-grade parents, what the expectations are and the routines for homework. So the next year it's a lot easier because they know what to expect. For instance, all my kids buy binders to organize themselves. They know that in fourth grade they're going to use them and in fifth grade they're going to use them. And the parents get into the routine for that. I think routines in people's crazy lives are really important, and that's one really important thing that multiage [teaching] gives parents."

Jodi Lane: "Every time that a child goes to a new teacher from year to year, there's a certain amount of stress for the child and for the parent. And I think that it [multiage schooling] takes away that stress for a year. They think, 'Oh, yeah, we know how it's going to be.' I think it makes life a little easier sometimes. I have such strong parent support in the classroom. At the beginning of this year, right from the first week of school, I had parents from last year say, 'When can we come in?' And they were able to start coming in that first and second week, whereas with the parents that I didn't quite know yet, I wanted to wait until we had an opportunity to talk and discuss what their role would be in the classroom. So I think for those parents, there wasn't that lag time either, as well as for the kids. They were able to get right back into it and not have to wait around for anything."

Alice Leeds: "For parents, they really get to know the teacher. I think that's a big plus. They know who is with their kid every day, all day long. And they get to develop a certain comfort level, so if there is a touchy subject or if they're concerned about something, they can talk. I've had parents talk to me about things that were good for me to be aware of but that may have been difficult for them to talk about. You just develop more of an ease. I've worked with parents over three years who've had challenging situations at home, and you develop a whole rapport around their kid. They don't have to readjust every year and think, 'Well, how is it going to be for my child this year, and what's the teacher going to expect, what kind of homework is there going to be, what are they going to do about this, that, and the other?' They get to know what the story is. So just the way the child gets comfortable, the parents can get comfortable. And if there are some things that they're not comfortable with, usually they're worked out in the first year; and from there, it's smooth sailing."

Carol Hasson: "I think that when you only have a student for one year, it's really hard to notice any big—except every once in a while—academic progress. It's hard to see where kids started and where they ended, unless you really document all along the way. And even then, in one year, it's hard to see a lot of progress. Sometimes parents are the ones that see their child making that progress more than teachers do, and parents are feeling more positive than teachers do at the end of certain periods of time in the kid's life and say, 'Wow, this is where they were, and this is where they are.' And I think that, having a child for more than one year, you can share the enthusiasm with the parent and say, 'Gosh, remember two years ago when so-and-so came in my room, and here's a piece of work that they were doing then. And now here it is two years later, and, wow, look at this book that they started reading, and now look what kind of books they can read!' I think that is really positive, because parents know now that you can see that and appreciate it more than you could when you only had their child for one year."

DISADVANTAGES OF MULTIAGE CLASSROOMS

> *I think [the multiage approach] is easier for the teacher, because if the teacher's busy, some sixth grader or somebody who knows could go and help a kid that needs help.*
>
> —Fifth-grade student in 4/5/6 multiage classroom

Are there losses or disadvantages in multiage classrooms for children? Absolutely none, each of these teachers said.

What about for teachers?

"It's a lot of work," John Bourgoin said. "It's a tremendous amount of work."

"It's a lot more work at the start," Debbie Cross said. "And later on it's still more work than straight grades are."

"Every year is different," Arnell Paquette explained. "We thought after the third year [that] we'd go into our fourth year, which would be repeating the first year, and we'd have it made. Well, it wasn't anything like our first year. So every year has been different, and that's because of the class and the makeup. And that's both a challenge and a lot of work."

Pat Minor's perspective on the workload was a bit different: "It does take a lot of preparation time. And the first year I worked on this, it took a while. I guess anytime you switch grade levels or add a grade, you don't have the materials necessarily that you might need for extending the ranges that you might have. So it takes a while to build up the reading books and the manipulatives, that kind of thing. Sometimes having to extend, having things that we do open-ended so they will take in all of the ranges of ability, takes some work. This is the fourth year, so I'm finding less problems pulling out materials that I've used and adding to them. I think after the initial shock in trying to figure out how to deal with the ranges that you've got, I don't think it's that much different in a lot of ways."

"Parents don't always understand the benefits at first," Alice Leeds noted. "So I think it's important to share with parents and encourage their understanding of the benefits. That can be somewhat challenging. On the positive side, parents sell the idea of multiage [teaching] to each other just as the children do. This year a group of concerned parents worked with a couple of teachers in our school to evaluate our multiage program, and they were really turned around. They've become our best spokespeople for multiage [classes]."

Finally, Leeds identified one unanticipated negative: "Well, you do feel more of a commitment. You can look at this as a negative or a positive. You feel more of a commitment to your kids. For me to think about leaving at any point, if I would ever think about leaving, I would be leaving some kids midstream. I would always feel like I was leaving in the middle of the year. So you make a bigger commitment to a school when you become a multiage teacher. You're making a bigger commitment to a group of children. And that's a responsibility that you take on as a multiage teacher. You really feel like if you leave, you need to help bridge that transition. It's never a great time to leave."

Are there losses or disadvantages in multiage classrooms for parents? None of these teachers articulated any.

"I know concerns that parents have," Jodi Lane noted, "but I haven't seen any negatives or had any parents tell me about anything like that."

Leeds commented, "Of course, if a parent is having a problem with the teacher, I think if they're anxious, then they get more anxious. They think, 'Oh, gosh, I'm going to have to deal with this teacher for two or three years.' Parents, I think, are more likely to come up early on and try to get it worked out. They're not as likely to wait it out. So it might seem negative, but my experience is that it ends up being positive."

Teachers and parents, of course, aren't the only fans of multiage schooling. As illustrated by all of the students' comments throughout this chapter and by those below of several sixth graders who participated in a 4/5/6 multiage class, the advantages to the children are evident:

"I stayed with [teacher's name] three years, and she was nice. I got where I knew everything she would say. I could almost say it before she said it. She would look at me and she'd go, 'You been with me in this class so long!' That was really nice."

"The younger kids depend on the older kids a lot. And sometimes the older kids depend on the younger ones, because it's pretty amazing what some of them can do. Some of them, you think, 'Oh man, they don't know that question.' But then a lot of them know it. That's pretty amazing. . . . The younger kids really do look up to us, because if they need help or something, they're always asking an older kid."

"I was in a regular fourth grade in [another state]. I like the multiage better. It's more like different people—kinda different people have to learn to get along good, and they do!"

10

THE ACADEMIC BENEFITS OF ELEMENTARY MULTIAGE CLASSROOMS

In dozens of interviews that I have conducted with multiage teachers in Vermont, Maine, Washington, Oregon, and British Columbia over the past decade, I've heard a familiar refrain when it comes to the academic benefits of multiage classrooms. Multiage teachers as a group are convinced that multiage classrooms generate three sets of academic benefits:

- Students in multiage classrooms score at least as well as their peers in single-grade classrooms on standardized tests, whether norm referenced or criterion referenced. In many cases—or perhaps most—they score higher.
- Almost all students in multiage classrooms identify topics or subjects that hold significant personal interest and meaning to them. Through their investigation of these topics, students become knowledgeable and expert about a body of information and understanding, and they begin to learn about authentic values and uses of knowledge in human life.
- Because students in multiage classrooms become engaged in inquiry about topics and subjects of interest to them, they become both skilled as researchers and learners *and* competent at explaining what they know to others.

Unfortunately, no one has conducted the kind of large-scale, longitudinal, and multiattribute study that is needed to support these beliefs in social scientific terms. For that matter, even a large-scale study based on only standardized test data has never been conducted.

Recall the Student Teacher Achievement Ratio (STAR) inquiry in Tennessee. The STAR project involved 7,000 students in seventy-nine schools over a four-year period, and its results have provided convincing research support for the clear superiority of primary-grade classes with fifteen to seventeen children. This is the scope of study that is needed if we are ever to examine multiage classrooms through the lens of social science in a way that could generate sufficiently complex and convincing data.

Without this kind of study, the best research results available lie in Barbara Nelson Pavan's examination of sixty-four studies of multiage (or nongraded) elementary classes published between 1968 and 1990. In 58 percent of the studies, students in multiage classes scored higher on standardized tests than did the students in the control single-grade classes. In 33 percent of the studies, students in multiage and single-grade classes scored the same. In only 9 percent of the studies did students in the single-grade classes score higher on the standardized measures than the multiage students. Pavan and Robert Anderson, the coauthor of her 1993 book *Nongradedness,* call these results "a substantial and generally favorable body of research on nongradedness."[1]

Robert Slavin and Roberto Gutierrez examined fifty-seven pertinent studies that met their criteria for good research.[2] They found that students in multiage (or nongraded) classrooms scored higher, again on standardized tests, in 35 percent of these studies. In contrast, students in single-grade classrooms scored higher in only 5 percent of the studies. There were no significant differences in scores in the remaining studies.

In addition, Slavin and Gutierrez note that the studies of nongraded classes that they cite fall into four distinct categories of educational programs: Joplin-like programs (in which students are regrouped in a nongraded way for particular subjects; named after a model program in Joplin, Missouri); comprehensive (in which the classroom that Alice Leeds describes in part 1 of this book would fit, as well as all of the other multiage classrooms described in this volume); and two versions of individualized instruction. These authors note that in their review of pertinent studies, the classrooms employing the Joplin-like and comprehensive approaches to nongradedness produced consistently higher scores than the individualized approaches. Indeed, the Joplin-like programs, which most multiage teachers would not see as "real multiage," had a higher median effect size (+.46) than did the comprehensive classes (+.34). But eight of the fourteen studies of nongraded or multiage comprehensive classes showed positive outcomes that were statistically significant, while only four of the nine Joplin-like program studies displayed positive results of this sort. While Slavin and Gutierrez conclude in this analysis that their findings most strongly support the Joplin-like nongraded model, one can find equally strong support in their data for what they call "comprehensive" programs—a multiage classroom that integrates student interest and initiative with teacher leadership and focus, a classroom like that described by Leeds in this volume and just about all of those analyzed in teacher-authored publications on multiage teaching throughout the 1990s.

Anne Bingham, in *Exploring the Multiage Classroom*, notes that Anderson and Pavan "included seventeen longitudinal studies, of which 69% favored nongraded settings, suggesting that the advantages of such settings increase with the time spent in them."[3] Elizabeth Lolli conducted a three-year study in California, comparing multiage to single-grade classes, and she concluded that "the longer students remained in multiage classrooms, the better the results. Children who were behind their peers when they entered the multiage class caught up to those peers by the third year of testing."[4]

Wendy Kasten and Barbara Clarke studied a group of children in a Florida multiage program from the start of kindergarten to the end of what would have been their third-grade year. Kasten and Clarke found that "children in multiage settings . . . had actual mean scores higher than their (single grade) counterparts on all subtests (on the National Achievement Test and the Stanford Achievement Test) but only those in thinking skills, math computation, math concepts, and using information on the Stanford Achievement Tests were significantly higher."[5]

So what can we claim about academic achievement in multiage classrooms in light of this examination of the research?

- A very strong case can be made that children in elementary multiage classrooms will score at least as well on standardized tests as they would have in single-grade classrooms.

- A strong but not absolutely convincing case can be made that a majority of children in elementary multiage classrooms will score significantly higher on standardized tests than they would have in single-grade classrooms.

- So much of what is most important in children's learning—about their own intellectual interests and capacities, about the relationships between interest and learning in children's learning, about children's ability to gain expert knowledge in a topic of their choosing, about their ability to convey expert knowledge to others, and about children's experience of their own efficacy as learners and experts—is central to life in multiage classrooms and is not at all measured by standardized tests. But we know that multiage teachers consistently describe the success of many or most children in their classrooms at becoming self-motivated and competent learners.

To go beyond our current reliance on limited test data and teachers' self-reports, we need a multiage research program that has the depth and resources of the STAR project and that will investigate, with a large enough sample of students over a long enough period of time, the whole range of issues involved in the academic benefits of multiage classrooms.

NOTES

1. R. H. Anderson and B. Nelson Pavan, *Nongradedness: Helping It to Happen* (Lancaster, Pa.: Technomic Press, 1993), p. 53.
2. R. Gutierrez and R. Slavin, "Research in Nongraded Elementary Schools," in R. Fogarty, ed., *Think about Multiage Classrooms: An Anthology of Original Essays* (Palatine, Ill.: IRI Skylight Publishing, 1995), p. 64.
3. A. Bingham, with P. Dorta, M. McClaskey, and J. O'Keefe, *Exploring the Multiage Classroom* (York, Maine: Stenhouse, 1995), p. 10.
4. W. C. Kasten and E. Lolli, *Implementing Multiage Education: A Practical Guide* (Norwood, Mass.: Christopher-Gordon Publishers, 1998), p. 22.
5. Ibid.

III

SUCCEEDING AT MULTIAGE TEACHING

⓫

MULTIAGE CLASSROOMS AND STATE STANDARDS AND TESTING

By 2001, almost every state in the United States had instituted its own version of the same statewide curriculum standards and high-stakes testing system that had been urged upon the states through the combined forces of corporate leaders such as Louis Gerstner of RJR Nabisco and later IBM and Frank Shrontz of Boeing, Presidents George Bush (the elder) and Bill Clinton, and education secretaries Lamar Alexander and Richard Riley. Given the enormous political power of these forces, almost every state had fallen in line, even though no single state has actually demonstrated the efficacy of this intensified industrial model of centralized educational control.

Most multiage teachers I know were both wary of increased centralization of curricula and opposed to intensified standardization of schooling. At the same time, all multiage teachers clearly supported the announced goals of the standards-and-testing model, which focused on raising academic achievement for all students, particularly for young people who were currently failing in school. But most multiage teachers were concerned by the ways in which this new model's dependence on standardized tests for measurement could lead to "teaching to the test" in many classrooms, to an impoverishment of the curriculum in their own classrooms, and possibly to the systematic removal of multiage classrooms from public schools.

What has become evident in recent years is that as far as their effects on multiage classrooms, not all state standards-and-testing systems have similar implications.

- Some states have implemented a system in which their standards are focused heavily on the recall or identification of information. Many or most of these states have also put in place an assessment system that primarily or exclusively employs multiple choice or other objective question formats.
- Some states have put in place standards that are more broadly focused on skills, understandings, and the ability to use information. Many or most of these states have implemented assessment systems that employ some or many test items that are performance based and require writing, problem solving, investigations, and/or some other open-ended student response.
- Some states have an assessment system in which students are tested each and every year. Some states even require students to pass a single high-stakes test each year to go on to the next grade. Other states deploy their tests at strategic points along the path from kindergarten to high school graduation, for example, at fourth, seventh, and tenth grades.

Given the few years of experience we've had now with new standards-and-testing systems, it seems evident that multiage classrooms of the sort described in this volume can not only survive, but can actually prosper in some of these standards-and-testing environments; in others, multiage classrooms become almost impossible.

- If the state standards are focused on facts, and if testing occurs on a yearly basis, then the kind of multiage classroom described herein cannot be enacted if scoring highly on the state test is a goal for the students.
- If the state standards are focused on understandings and skills, or if the state standards integrate a reasonable amount of key facts with understandings and skills, then there is an opening for the use of multiage classrooms.
- However, even with the latter kind of standards, if the state tests students each and every year with the expectation of the same amount of learning for all students during the previous year, it will be diffi-

cult to prepare students to score well on these kinds of annual tests within a multiage framework. By definition, multiage as a concept recognizes the variability in the development and learning of different children and frames this variation not as a problem, but as an opportunity. State curriculum standards and testing systems that expect all children to learn the same things in the same year of their lives display a profound ignorance of human development and a contempt for the uniqueness of individual human beings.

- If standards are focused on understandings and skills, or if the state standards integrate key facts with understandings and skills *and* with a regimen of testing that is spaced strategically over the thirteen years of schooling, multiage classrooms can thrive. In such classrooms, the vast majority of students can master the learning targets set by the state to the desired level of accomplishment—and they can develop the qualities and abilities as learners and human beings described throughout this volume and in the many other books about multiage classrooms written by multiage teachers in the past decade.

In the latter kind of standards-and-testing environment, multiage teachers can draw on their multiyear relationship with students. First, they know their students well as individuals; thus they have rich data about what each child knows and can do—and what she/he needs yet to learn and master. Second, multiage teachers have more time in which to help a student meet any particular standard. The teacher can set long-range goals for individual students over a two- or three-year expanse, engage students in learning focused on their own personal goals, and carefully monitor students' progress over time. A multiage classroom allows the teacher to attend to individual learners in a much more focused way than she/he could in a single year.

A multiage classroom also supports students' learning to meet standards in other ways:

- The multiage classroom encourages a spiraling curriculum in which the teacher can return to particular academic standards with increasing levels of sophistication over time, both in a single academic year and from one year to the next.
- The multiage classroom is a place where learning is supported and deepened through the qualities of community created by teacher

and students. These community-oriented qualities make the multi-age classroom an ideal place to ask children to reach toward higher academic standards, because they have so much support for and acknowledgment of learning in such a classroom, not only from the teacher, but also from their peers.

- The multiage classroom provides an opportunity for the teacher to develop student leaders who are knowledgeable and adept in specific areas of the curriculum. The multiage teacher can factor this peer support into her/his curricular planning and engage competent students in assisting their peers with specific academic standards.

The responses and concerns of multiage teachers in this "better-case" standards-and-testing environment—which currently exists, imperfectly but to a significant extent, in Washington State—are exemplified in the three comments that follow, each of which was shared with me by a veteran multiage teacher:

"I feel there is merit to the EALRs [Essential Academic Learning Requirements, Washington State's academic standards] and the WASL [Washington Assessment of Student Learning, the state's test, currently given in fourth, seventh, and tenth grades; about 40 percent performance based]. I'm not sure we have them correct yet; there are still things that need to be worked out. I think if we view the EALRs as targets for kids to reach within an appropriate period of time, they can be helpful. We also need not to judge success only by one measure, the WASL, but we need to use several measures: projects, work samples, portfolios, etc. If we use the EALRs and the WASL in this way, we can help all children to be successful. But if we get too specific about some EALRs being for some grades and you need to get them before you go on, then we'll take away the possibility of multiage teaching."

"I think the reading, writing, listening, and math EALRs set high standards and goals to strive for. . . . I think the WASL for reading in fourth grade is difficult but fair. But I think the WASL for math in fourth grade is too difficult for these children. But even so, because I teach my students for three years (the equivalent of grades 1–3), I feel a tremendous responsibility for them to do well on the fourth-grade tests. And in those three years, I can help them come a long way toward doing that."

"I believe the EALRs provide us with useful academic targets. And if they were disconnected from their grade-level connections, they'd provide a good continuum of learning. But with the WASL, more and more I see an emphasis in my district on the test rather than on student learning. Pressure to do well on the WASL seems to be causing administrators to want to adopt curricula that are scripted and allow for little teacher modification. Of course, this type of curriculum is deadly to multiage classes, where diversity is embraced and students are measured by their own progress."

As illustrated by this Washington State example, much of the fate of the multiage approach will depend not only on how the standards are written and what kind of testing is conducted, but also on how well multiage teachers can advocate for and demonstrate the efficacy of the multiage model for educating children in the twenty-first century.

⑫

BECOMING A
MULTIAGE TEACHER

I interviewed nine teachers on a regular basis during the first three years of their work in multiage classrooms. All of these teachers were veterans who had volunteered to create multiage classrooms. The least experienced of the group was starting her ninth year in the classroom as she took on her first multiage assignment; the most veteran was beginning her nineteenth year. The others ranged from having thirteen to eighteen years of teaching experience. Of the nine teachers— seven females and two males—eight had chosen to teach in two-person teams and one was teaching alone. Two were teaching multiage grades 1/2/3; two were teaching multiage grades 2/3; and five were teaching multiage grades 4/5/6.

These teachers all taught in the Sunnyslope Community School, a public elementary school in Port Orchard, Washington, a partly suburban, partly exurban, partly rural community south of Bremerton on the Kitsap peninsula, across Puget Sound from Seattle. These nine teachers constituted a little less than half of the school's faculty.

What follows is a portrait of these nine teachers' first three years of multiage teaching, drawn with their own words. It is a portrait that illustrates in rich detail their aspirations and challenges, their struggles and accomplishments. The teachers' comments are labeled in two ways. Some quotes are used to convey experiences and perceptions common to most of the teachers, and these are included without identification of the speaker. Other comments are labeled with the speaker's name because they offer a more personal insight.

EARLY OCTOBER, FIRST YEAR

What do you hope to gain by creating a multiage classroom?

All nine teachers offered very similar responses to this question, which fit into four categories:

- To better serve the learning needs of students as individuals. Children can learn at their own levels, without the limitations of grade-based curricula. Children can go as far as they can with their learning.
- To develop stronger relationships and bonds with children and give them more caring, stability, and safety, which will support the learning and growth of all children, particularly those who have the least support at home.
- To challenge myself to grow as a teacher who does more than "teach to the middle of the class"; to become a teacher who can regularly assess the needs of each student as an individual and provide appropriate challenge and support; to develop a sense of stewardship for each child's growth over two or three years.
- To encourage and help children to integrate and use their knowledge and apply their skills sooner and more realistically than we usually allow in single-grade classes.

How have you prepared yourself for multiage teaching?

In response to this question, the teachers explained that as a result of the strong support they had received from their principal, they had devoted time toward this preparation during the two previous school years.

Year One: Reading articles and discussing them with colleagues; observing multiage classrooms in neighboring schools and discussing multiage issues with the teachers in those classrooms.

Year Two: More observations in multiage classrooms in the region; networking with a greater number of multiage teachers via e-mail, telephone, informal visits, workshops; reading articles and books; and taking professional development workshops and classes. Furthermore, the nine soon-to-be multiage teachers held discussions among themselves in their own school, and they prepared the curriculum and classroom structure and management with teaching partner or alone (over the summer): thematic units, physical setup of classroom, skill instruction, assessment, record keeping. Setup of new multiage classrooms occurred in August.

How are things going in your classroom now?

The following quotes identify five categories into which most of the teachers' responses fit.

"Right now teaching is demanding more time than I had to put in last year." "I'm working all day and taking things home, too. Some early mornings and some late afternoons. But it's starting to ease some already. Most of that workload is individualization."

"We're not labeling our students by grade. And some of the children—I don't know if they're first grade or second grade unless I get the class list out and look it up. It's not evident, and in here it's not important." "If someone watched us, you couldn't tell who was a fourth grader or a fifth grader or a sixth grader in this room. It's just not an issue."

"I'm starting to see kids take off in this new kind of classroom. So far we've focused on teaching them how to do things here, and just this week they're really starting to take off."

"It's a lot more fun than I thought it was going to be. I knew it was going to be a lot of work, and it is, and I knew about the rewards for children—but I didn't expect that the rewards for myself were going to be just as large."

"I have a lot more knowledge about how the children learn because we start out each day with a choice time. . . . So I can see what they choose and how they work and what their interests are. And I can see strengths in students in ways that I never had the opportunity to know before."

What is challenging for you right now?

Kelly Best (grades 4/5/6): "I have set the program up for students to be independent, to make choices about how to spend their time . . . and they're not real good at that just yet. So I need to help them develop the skills to do this. . . . And I need to get more structure so that I can keep them accountable, and myself, while they become more independent."

Diana Holmlund (grades 2/3): "My goal is to do a better job of tracking students' skills and needs. I'd like to develop a more efficient way to keep records of the assessment, both formal and informal, that I'm doing, especially the informal. I'm not comfortable with the system I'm currently using. I think better planning of lessons and activities will result in better record keeping."

Cathy Hulet (grades 2/3): "Making sure that I'm meeting the needs of all of my students. We're having a lot of fun, and it looks wonderful, but is every child getting what they need from me?"

Ginny Semler (grades 1/2/3): "Keeping on top of the curriculum. We have the units planned, so I know where we are going. . . . It's just making sure that I have enough materials in each unit for the whole gamut of reading levels. And that I have materials for reinforcement and enrichment."

Sharon Tankersley (grades 1/2/3): "One thing that's frustrating is that almost every time you turn around, there's another memo from the district saying first graders must do this, second graders must do this, and so on. . . . We're not labeling our kids by grade, but the district is."

Debbie Snowden (grades 4/5/6): "We're working on the systems for keeping track of kids' papers and for our record keeping."

Tom LaFerriere (grades 4/5/6): "The first month has been exhausting. Some days I wonder about this, but most days I'm an optimist. I know it's going to be worth it, it's going to be what I hope it will be. I just need to be patient."

Dave Matheny (grades 4/5/6): "Since we're team teaching completely and we have all the kids together, the challenge is to get to know all fifty-seven of the kids as individuals, to get some sense of intimacy in the classroom."

Vicki Voorhees (grades 4/5/6): "Right now the most challenging thing is making sure that we're meeting all of the [district] Student Learning Outcomes and adequately preparing these students. . . . Because we'll have them for three years, there's a lot more responsibility to make sure they are totally prepared for junior high."

MID-NOVEMBER, FIRST YEAR

How have things been going in the past month?

"Things are going more smoothly now. We've made a lot of little but continuous adjustments in the classroom, and we're getting both the curriculum and the organizational things more in a flow."

"What stands out for me now is that I work with small groups of children based on what their needs are at that moment, where I used to pick out a skill from the curriculum and teach it to the whole class."

"The kids are starting to pick other kids to work with based on criteria other than who their friends are. They're expanding out to work with other kids based on who they think knows what."

What is challenging for you now?

"Structuring math instruction to accommodate the wide range of skills."

"Staying ahead of the kids in developing the whole wide range of curricular materials for use in the centers and projects."

"Making sure the children who need direct instruction and skill instruction are getting enough of what they need."

"Getting enough assessment done for each child in all the core curricular areas."

What is rewarding for you now?

"Seeing the children of different ages work together so well."

"There's so much of students taking on responsibility for things, students taking the initiative."

"The older kids look at the younger kids almost like a mirror, because they can see by comparison how much they have grown, how much they have learned and can do."

Are there any lessons or insights for you so far?

Vicki Voorhees: "I'm seeing the truth of what can happen when I turn over more to my students . . . there's more freedom of choice, there's more room for movement. . . . We have three sixth graders whom I had last year who were nonachievers, nonworkers; school was not for them. Now they are writing, they're publishing mini-books, they're enthusiastic. . . . We're putting the learning in the hands of the students, and they are eager learners."

Kelly Best: "The lesson I'm learning is, just make sure you have the wide range of curricular materials that you need. I guess there's no way to have enough in the very first year. It's a challenge. But if you know the theme units you plan to teach before the year starts, you can just collect as much material for them as you can."

Ginny Semler: "You need to allocate enough time to make sure that you plan, because it's the planning, the preparation, that makes the day run smoothly. We planned for the fall before the school year started, and now we're planning for after Christmas. This really helps!"

Cathy Hulet: "It's going to take time to get your class to be really cohesive. Don't expect too much too soon, but it's starting to come together. It takes time."

Tom LaFerriere: "I feel like I'm on a journey of discovery. So I'm still testing out what I think I'm learning. I'm probably going to keep testing for a while."

Debbie Snowden: "When you need to level [or group] students for teaching specific skills, get your kids involved in leveling themselves. It's empowerment for them to make their own choices. Nobody feels like you've done anything to them. . . . I haven't heard anybody say, 'I'm in the high group' or 'I'm in the low group.' It's just, 'I'm in this group for this purpose.'"

LATE JANUARY, FIRST YEAR

What is your perspective on your multiage classroom now at midyear?

"We're seeing the development of all kinds of talents in our students, and it's particularly noticeable in our fourth and fifth graders—talents that we believe would not have been so evident otherwise."

"My kids are so blended now that you can't pick the second graders from the third graders. It's all become very individualized in terms of what they can do and what I expect from them."

"I think I'm meeting individual needs of kids better than I was last year, even though the range is greater. It's because of the way we have set up the room and the curriculum—and because of the way I see things differently."

"The kids have so much freedom in this kind of classroom. And I do, too. I feel much more at ease, like I have my own agenda. And we're doing so much more than my classes ever did before."

"The kids are constantly bringing in things that they've done over the weekend that connect with their projects in class. It's nothing I've thought of, they just do it. They take off and go from there, because they feel like they're a part of it. That's connected to their getting to make a good number of decisions in class."

"We've gotten really good support from parents. We had a few parents who were questioning, but they've all seen how really well this works for their own kids."

"I feel that we're meeting our students' academic needs much better than I was last year. I think their academic needs are met better through individualization, and socially they're becoming a lot more aware of and tolerant of differences in people."

"I feel more freedom to have the kids be part of everything. They make a lot more decisions on how we're going to study something, so they feel so much ownership in it that they want to take it to a higher level."

"Kids come off the bus, and we have 'output' for the first twenty minutes. They pick a station, and they really get into it. It's loud and there's lots of movement—it's free choice—but they're into the learning, not going off or playing around."

"Almost all of my students have learned how to work well at the centers. There are only a couple who are still struggling."

"We see less competition of the kind that is rivalries for attention or kids trying to top someone else or put them down, much less of this competition. The kind of competition we see more of is a healthy competition of this group versus another group for some fun activity."

"We've opened up the curriculum to kids' choices. . . . We say, 'Here's the topic and the lesson, look at a couple of things, and come if you want to give it a try.' Kids are remarkably accurate in terms of placing themselves, and they don't hesitate to put themselves in a tougher math group or literature group if that's what seems right to them."

"We're starting to think about developing the culture and continuity of our classroom from this first year into next year, and we're starting to talk with our kids about this."

What's challenging you now?

"The possibility of burnout: too much time at school, too much time thinking about school, too many things I don't get to do."

"The teaming has taken so much time. Of course, we do that to ourselves, because we don't seem to know when to stop. Two perfectionists on a team is scary."

"I have to learn to prioritize better, because I can't do everything that I can think of that might be worth doing."

"The fear that if I make a mess [with a child], I can really harm that child's life. That's a lot of responsibility. But most of the time, I feel more relieved by knowing that I have three years with each child to bring them along than I feel stressed by being so responsible."

"I'd like to have time now to reflect on what I'm doing—and to talk with some veteran multiage teachers. Now that I'm doing multiage, I have new questions and new ideas."

"I'm still struggling with having enough materials, having enough curriculum stuff for the wide range of fourth to sixth graders."

"I'm working on refining all the procedures, all the structures, in my classroom. I'll get there, but there's only so much change the kids will tolerate."

EARLY MARCH, FIRST YEAR

What's going on for you now?

"This is the best thing we've ever done for our students as far as learning goes. We've rethought a lot of our teaching to put more responsibility for learning in our students' hands. So we act more as guides, helpers, resources."

"We still have to meet the [district's] Student Learning Objectives, so you still have to get that in, but the delivery is entirely different from what we've done before. There's very little of this whole-class, frontal teaching to the middle."

"I think we're doing content in a lot more depth. I know we'll have most of these kids again next year, so I'm not worried so much about getting through everything to get them ready to go on. What they are ready to do now, this is what we are going to focus on."

"We're seeing a real growth in our special education students. We think that's a combination of [the] multiage [approach] and inclusion. . . . These [special education] kids blend in better in [a] multiage [setting]; they don't stick out because there's such a wide variation in work levels all around them. So these kids have a chance to feel like they're a part of everything like everyone else."

"It's been good for the older children to see what the younger kids can do. They're very compassionate and supportive, and I've never seen that so much in a single-grade class. We see a lot of kids helping each other and cheering each other on, without any involvement on our part."

"There's not the usual competition in our multiage classroom. The kids know that people are different, that there's this continuum. It's that people aren't all ready to do whatever it is all at the same time. So there's no stigma attached; it's not a race."

"I think the amount of time that we're working has decreased some. And it's become a lot less stressful as far as the planning goes."

"We had a conversation with a mom at a conference, and she said, 'My son is a fifth grader, and I want you to retain him.' We just kind of looked at each other in shock, and then we realized, we don't have to deal with that now. We're going to have him for another year, so we get more time to get him ready for junior high."

What are the issues that you're working on now?

"We're working on how to do conferences and report cards. We need to be more efficient, but also take advantage of how much we know together about each child and where he is."

"It's not that it's not still challenging. It is. But in the last few weeks, it's like we get these moments when we seem to come up for air. We're ready to go—everything is ready—and we still have time left before the kids arrive or before we need to go in the afternoon. It's a kind of shock."

LATE APRIL, FIRST YEAR

"It's been interesting to watch kids take more leadership. They really feel in charge of themselves and their learning in this environment. It's not the teachers' room, it's their room. It's not me giving them a grade; they really feel that they've earned whatever they get. They feel responsible. We can see that so clearly whenever we get a new student. They aren't empowered in the way that kids are who have been with us all year. The new kids want us to tell them what to do, where to be at first."

"I'm really starting to understand what continuous progress means. I thought I knew it, of course, before this year. But now it's real, not just a theory. I can say to kids, 'It's okay that we don't know this now. We can do it next year.' And they say, 'Okay, that sounds good.' We're just going to keep going. And I had one boy who would be a fifth grader who is going to finish all of fifth- and sixth-grade math by the end of this year. And he came to me, he wasn't being negative, but he was worried about math next year. So I told him we'd have lots for him to do, the prealgebra stuff and then maybe starting into algebra. So it's that you just keeping moving the kid on to what's next. I've never really done that before."

"I'm starting to really understand that I'm not going to have to start all over in the fall with a new group of kids. . . . I'm going to take a break and then pick up where we left off in June with most of these kids. And with some new kids who will join us. And some of my fourth- and fifth-grade students who will be returning are just beginning to figure this out, too."

"We're still refining the timing of things during the day, the routines and procedures and all that. We're also working more with centers than we did before, and the kids needed some time to get used to making those choices and then moving to the next center in the middle of the hour. We created some rubrics for how the room should be when they move and when they're at the centers, and that's helped a lot."

"My [teaching] partner and I are talking about some of the thematic units that we want to do next year. So we're starting to do some long-term planning for how we can better put those units together in this kind of classroom."

"We've made a lot of progress with the report cards and conferences from the first efforts at these. There's more we need to figure out, but we've already gotten these to be manageable and very useful for the kids."

"It seems like we've been doing this for more than one year because everything is just flowing now."

"The way that I do my planning now and the way that I teach have changed so radically from the traditional way that I was taught to teach. I can't imagine going back to what I used to do."

"We're seeing the evidence of kids' learning in our multiage [classroom]. We're already seeing it this spring. I thought it would take until the second year at least, but it's there right now, both the academic skills and the way that kids are learning to be responsible for their own learning."

"I had a mother in class yesterday helping out. She was worried in the fall that we wouldn't challenge her son enough. Now she was able to point out specific things in [the] multiage [setting] that had encouraged him. . . . She said, 'You have been able to challenge him and enrich him and make him excel beyond what I thought was possible.' And I realized that I had done that way beyond what I had thought possible."

"I don't know why I couldn't have been teaching this way in my regular sixth-grade class. Part of it is the mind-set that just gets locked in: sixth graders do this, they do that. But in multiage, you have such a wide range that you can't say that multiage kids do this. So it's like breaking the mold and opening up all these possibilities for kids."

"Now we're still putting in a little more time than we were last year, and mostly that's time we need to talk with each other. But we get out at a decent time now, we don't feel overworked or overloaded. . . . Even at the start of the year, it wasn't too bad. I think it's because we prepared so well last summer and we were so organized and we had our systems figured out."

"Some of the kids who were not so tolerant in the fall have become much more tolerant of differences, and even accepting. And the 'special needs' kids have all developed at least some friendships with the 'regular' kids. That's really heartening for me to see."

"One of the second graders who was a nonreader in the fall read a book aloud yesterday—she wanted to do it. And the kids clapped and cheered for her. They were really on her side and helping her to note her progress."

"I don't feel the kind of intense push I've always felt at this point in the school year: 'It's near the end and I've got to get through these eighteen things, or else I've failed these kids.' We look at this as a three-year commitment, and so we have lessened the amount of rushed curriculum coverage we do and we've done a much more thorough job of teaching what we have studied."

"The pressure I feel now is about math. We need to do a better job of keeping up with tracking where each kid is in math so we can work with them where they need the work."

"The older kids are such good leaders now, and I know it's helped them to be better leaders because of having the younger kids in the class. I remember teaching third grade alone—but these third graders in my multiage [class] are so much more able and confident as leaders."

"When I was teaching before this year, I taught the whole group mostly. Now I can see how little I looked at individuals to see where they were, although at the time, I didn't see what I wasn't doing. Now I'm always looking at each kid and asking myself, 'Where is she now, and what does she need next?'"

"I'm still working more than I was last year, but I'm used to it now. And I'm a lot more rewarded for my time now; things feel so much more rewarding."

"Of all my years of teaching, I'm liking this one best."

"I have one kid who—I'm just not getting through to this kid, it's not working. And this kid is in fourth grade. So I don't want to take the responsibility for having him for three years, not because I can't deal with him or he can't survive. But I'm saying that if we're missing the boat, you've got to see if there's someone who might do better with him. So I'm starting to talk about this with [the principal] and some of the other intermediate teachers. We need to see what's best."

"Multiage has raised my expectations for what I believe the older kids can do. When I see the fourth graders working in such a responsible way, I expect the older kids to do at least as well, if not more. It's not the level of the work itself—that I expect to vary from kid to kid. But it's how the kids handle the choices and responsibilities."

MID-JUNE, FIRST YEAR

Kelly Best: "The family atmosphere in the classroom, where there's such a willingness to help each other—that's the best thing about this year. The older kids have more leadership opportunities and the younger kids have role models. . . .

"The hardest thing has been preparing curriculum to meet all of the needs and trying to always be sensitive to the range of reading levels."

Sharon Tankersley: "It's amazing what the [special needs] kids have been exposed to and the help their peers have given them. For all the kids, we've adjusted the curriculum for what the kids are ready for right now. If you would have asked me back in the fall where some of the lower-skilled kids would be right now, I couldn't have imagined how far they would have come. And at the opposite end of the spectrum, we have some first-year students who are reading with the third graders. . . .

"I've also felt that we had much more control over our curriculum this year because we don't have to race through everything. . . . So we could do more in-depth studies. And we've had the time to teach things that we were excited to teach. . . .

"The most challenging part has been all the report cards and conferencing that comes with putting our two classes together and each one of us needing to be involved with each child."

Ginny Semler: "What's best for me this year is the amount the children have learned. We've learned how to work with the children where they are, and that makes so much difference in terms of how far we can help to bring them along.

"I'm looking for a very different year next year, because we'll have all these kids back again. We'll just have to see what it means. One year is too new to know."

Cathy Hulet: "The teaming part has been the best for me: teaming with my teaching partner and the kids teaming with each other and us. We've all learned how to work together, even when it's not always easy.

"The biggest challenge is the time commitment. I don't know if it gets better, if it's just been the first year. I hope so. That's what teachers said when we did our multiage classroom visits. In the classroom itself, the most challenging piece for me is keeping track so all the kids get what they need. I don't want to lose track of anyone."

Debbie Snowden: "My experience this year confirms for me that the younger kids can reach higher standards. I thought we were underestimating them some, and in [the] multiage [classroom], they have models to bring them up. And they did just that. . . . A lot of what we tried this year has been open-ended, and it's allowed kids to reach as far as they could—and so many kids have gone beyond what we expected, at all age levels.

"I need to get more in balance in my personal life. Both of us are very capable and we have all these ideas we want to try, but we need to do better at drawing the line. Not compromising the quality, but being more efficient and not trying to do everything now."

Tom LaFerriere: "I think the most valuable thing has been all the relationships that all of us, kids and teachers, have built this year. And I think that's only going to grow when we've been with kids for two and then three years.

"The hardest thing has been having the two classes together as one, having sixty kids in the room."

Dave Matheny: "One of the best things in our multiage [class] has been the empowerment for kids, that they were choosing so much for themselves—where they go at times and how they fit and who they work with. And they got to choose from their interests and their learning style. . . . I'm doing much less direct instruction, and the kids are teaching each other more. And it's not just the older kid teaching the younger; it goes both ways.

"We're still working on the structures in the classroom. Some of the kids are a little too free, and they don't get enough done. So we're working on that. . . . And we want to do assessment better. We want to immerse the kids and ourselves in assessment of their work in a more practical, useful way."

Vicki Voorhees: "The empowerment of our kids and how much their confidence has grown, that's what so striking to me. They'll get up in front of an audience and speak their part. They'll troubleshoot problems and take care of difficulties. We tell them what we're doing and what the guidelines are, and they just do it. . . . They don't hesitate to go to someone they know who is an expert in something to get help. And they don't hesitate to offer their help—they do it tactfully. There's a real sense of support. . . . And we've seen so many students develop talents this year that we didn't even know they had. They may have been weak academically before or they may have had a behavior problem, but in this multiage [class], they were in a different environment, and suddenly they're shining.

"We've taken a lot of risks with this multiage venture. Many of them have worked out well, but some have flopped. So I hope we don't sit back and get complacent."

Diana Holmlund: "My teaching has changed a lot this year. I'm working with the [district] Student Learning Objectives, but I'm focusing much more on each child as an individual learner."

A clear set of themes run through these teachers' comments from their first year of multiage teaching:

"It's more work than what I was doing last year."

"It is really motivating, really energizing for me, even though it's more work. It got me out of my routine and into a set of new and exciting challenges."

"It gives me more opportunities to teach about topics and themes that are of personal interest to me."

"I know more this year about individual students—their interests, passions, styles, capabilities, intelligences—than I did before, because I am giving students more opportunities to make choices and I am observing what they choose."

"Teaming is a lot of work, but it's rewarding and fun and good for kids, and we make better decisions together than I did alone."

"We are doing less coverage of curriculum and more in-depth study, with more choices within a theme."

"I'm using less whole-class instruction and more instruction with centers, stations, projects, and groups/pairs. There's much more activity and less sitting at desks."

"We're teaching individual children where they are, either individually or in groups. We're not teaching to the middle."

"We are giving more choice and responsibility to students for their own learning—and children are responding by becoming empowered and responsible."

"I feel a much greater sense of responsibility for each child's learning because I will be her/his teacher for three years."

"I've lost sight on a day-to-day basis of which grade each child would be in if he/she were in single-grade classes."

"I'm excited about keeping children in class for three years, about where these relationships can go and how far kids can go in their learning in that time."

"I'm happy not to have to worry about failing kids if I'm going to have them in class for another one or two years beyond this one. I feel like I'll have time to get them where they need to be."

"We're developing genuinely integrative, interdisciplinary units, so we can study topics in a lot more depth."

"On the whole, the time required for this kind of teaching has decreased over the year. And we're getting better at teaching this way."

"We continue to have conflicts with district policies that require kids to do things by grade level. This identification of kids by grade level interferes with our effort to remove grade levels from all of our heads."

"We need to keep working on our record-keeping systems for marking kids' progress, and we need to be sure that children who need direct skills instruction get enough of that from us in a timely manner."

OCTOBER, SECOND YEAR

In Washington State, about 80 percent of school funding comes from the state government. The remaining 20 percent is raised through local operating levies that must be passed by the voters every two or three years. At the end of the first year of multiage implementation at Sunnyslope Community School, the voters in this district failed to pass their operating levy, which led to significantly increased class sizes throughout the school.

As a result of these increased class sizes, one of the nine teachers from the first year of the multiage study returned to a single-grade class. Another started the year with a single-grade class and then was invited to teach a grades 1/2/3 multiage class that started up in mid-September. Two other teachers in the school started a teamed grades 2/3 multiage class. The comments below were offered by the seven teachers who continued their multiage programs from the first year.

What stands out for you now in October?

"We have such a large number of kids—sixty-four, and we only had fifty-six last year—it just takes up so much of our attention; . . . but the saving grace is that kids who have returned from last year are much more mature. They know what's going on, they're becoming the leaders. They're just coming forward, tuned in, and consistently doing good work."

"I love having the kids back whom we had before. I know several of our kids who had a history of having a bad time at the start of each new school year: new teacher, they've got to try out all the games they can play. But not now. They're just picking up where they left off in June. . . . But then, we have sixty-five kids. We had to make some changes that led to somewhat less child movement and somewhat more teacher movement. They have somewhat less freedom, but we haven't sacrificed the real stuff in our program."

"The parents from last year are very comfortable with us. I like being in a situation where the parent calls me by my first name, and that's what I call her. It's so much more relaxed."

"We had a problem because the new fourth graders—when they asked for help from the older kids, they wanted to get the answers. But the older kids wouldn't give them answers; they wanted to give them ideas about what to do next. And when the younger kids didn't want that, the older kids would just walk away. We had to talk to each group, the fourth graders here and the fifth and sixth graders there, about what giving and getting help meant. And now the fourth graders are getting it. And the older kids are more clear and more patient."

"We're in the second year of our three-year social studies curriculum sequence. U.S. history, Washington State history, and exploration of North America. We took all three years and laid it out as a three-year sequence. . . . I'm really enjoying the time we have. We're spending a week on each of the thirteen original colonies. That's so much more depth than doing the whole thing in two or three weeks."

"We had fifty-eight kids at first in our grades 1/2/3 multiage [class]. That was just crazy. Just crazy. Finally last week the school got funding for another class [the district made budget cuts in other programs to lower primary-grade class sizes], and now we're down to forty-one. It's just another world now. . . . Even when we had the fifty-eight, the children returning from last year knew the rules, they knew what was expected of them, and they taught the new kids. That really helped us out. But there was a lot we had planned that we couldn't do in September because we had too many kids in the room."

"I feel really close to the parents who are with us for a second year. . . . We've got several parents who give us support and who can explain how things work to other parents. When they've seen how [the] multiage [approach] can work for their child, they can do a better job of selling the program to another parent than we can."

"We planned much of the year's curriculum in the summer. But we spent less time than we did the previous summer, because we knew the layout this time for what we were trying to do."

"Even though I had half of my thirty kids who were new instead of the one-third that I had expected—we had a lot of new fourth graders, and some older kids moved—they just jumped right into work by the second day. I took the new kids aside and talked with them about the rules, but mostly they got it from the students who had returned. The returning kids guided the new kids."

"I feel more comfortable with what I'm doing this year. Even with the large class, I'm doing better with record keeping, with giving choices to students, with keeping up with everything. And I am spending less time working than I did last year; that's obvious and good news."

"Even with the size of the classes at sixty-four kids, this was the easiest start I've ever had, because more than half of our students were returning. They knew the procedures, the routines, all that. . . . We found we didn't need to go over everything with the whole group because the old kids had already taught the new kids. So we were off and running by the second day, even though we had twenty-six fourth graders."

"We have a little boy who didn't say ten words aloud all of last year. He comes in this year and he's talking. He tells us, 'I'm glad to be coming back to the same place.'"

"The older kids have stepped into their roles as leaders very well. They're really nice with the new kids. They're all very eager to be the one to show them the ropes and to teach them how we do things in this room."

LATE JANUARY, SECOND YEAR

"It [the multiage program] just meets kids' needs: academically, socially, psychologically, physically. . . . It lets us really individualize the program. I'm a lot more free in multiage to help children individually."

"The workload this year is about the same as last spring. We're on a three-year curriculum cycle, so we're still scrambling for a wide range of materials. We're beating the bushes. Let me tell you, this is the most expensive class I've taught."

"Having a child in class for the second year, you just know them so well. With just about all of the kids who returned, it's been great. But there's one little boy we've really done nothing with for two years. We've kept at it with all we know, and we seem to have had no effect on this child, and that's frustrating. Before, you said, 'Well I tried. I'll send him on, and maybe the next teacher will do better.' But with two years and no movement, it's very frustrating."

"With the moms for these kids who are back with us, we're all on a first-name basis now. There's a real closeness."

"We have these great lines of communication with the kids in their second year with us, and with their parents. The parents just seem more open, and some of that openness seems to have rubbed off on some of the first-year parents."

"There still isn't that much support for multiage in the district. They still want to fit us into their grade-level boxes for curriculum and special programs like DARE and health education. It's a struggle."

"I don't know if multiage is the best for all children. For most, well, yes. But if you take a kid who has been a traditional kind of outwardly directed high achiever, who dots the i's and crosses the t's and does it really well—these kids are high achievers, but they haven't internalized their motivation. They have a tough time in [the] multiage [classroom] because they don't know where the bar is that they have to get over, and the bar keeps moving. That can frustrate them."

"In the fall, when we had sixty-five kids, everything seemed out of control. Now we're down to sixty, and that seems manageable in comparison. But last year we had fifty-four, and if you had asked me about sixty, I would have said, 'No way.' According to our contract, we could go to sixty-eight kids. I can't even imagine that."

"With more kids, we've had to cut down on kids' choices. Right now kids' choices are more managed. We give them three options, for example, rather than a whole range, like we did last year. But we're working on how to increase the range of choices they have."

"I've gotten so much better this year at planning my lessons so that kids are doing the work for their learning. I'm giving them the directions, the framework, the resources—and they're off. It's not a formula, it's more complex than that. But they use their time researching, putting the ideas together, fitting in the details, having their work meet the objectives I give them. It's been something of an astonishment to me how well this works. . . . We're doing a unit now on fossils and geology, and, yes, of course, dinosaurs. And they're all doing their research and then sharing it with each other. I'm learning a good deal myself from what the kids have discovered."

"Sometimes we can see just how far we've already come. For example, last week we had visitors in class from another school, and they complimented us on how we handle some of the organizational stuff. And for us, wow, that was basic by now. We're off on some much more complex tangent so we can continue to get kids to do more for themselves."

"Even though there's a broader range of kids in multiage, a broader range of abilities than in regular, it continues to amaze me how much better I feel that we can meet their needs. . . . I think maybe it comes in part from a freedom from curriculum. Now we give ourselves permission to make the learning materials fit the child. It's not Billy who is a fifth grader but who needs to work with fourth-grade words and so he's behind—it's Billy who is reading these words, at this level, and we want him to read and read and he'll learn more words. It removes the stigma, and then there's no high group and low group. At times, we might have sixteen different things going on the room, and they're all good things."

"Sixty-four kids just fill up the physical space of the room. There's just too many bodies."

"I couldn't have nine reading groups in regular class. I couldn't manage it. But somehow here we have nine levels or twelve levels or whatever, because the kids just find each other when they're at the same place. And then they find someone who can help them or someone whom they can help. . . . It seems to me that these first and second graders are farther along academically than the kids I've taught before in first- and second-grade regular classes."

"We're stuck with the district curriculum. But we've laid out the science and social studies units on a continuum over three years."

JUNE, SECOND YEAR

Debbie Snowden: "Even with the increase in numbers, it's been a wonderful year. . . . I always felt before that I was either teaching the low kids well or the high kids, but I didn't feel I was doing the job at both ends. And that's the strongest part of multiage for me. This year we really did the job with everybody. . . .

"The kids who have been with us know what's going on. They can say, 'Remember when we did such-and-such last year? Well, that would work here.' So they're helping us to plan how we structure our activities."

Sharon Tankersley: "I feel that we know the families and we know the children so much better than in the past. We know just about all of the families on a first-name basis.

"I also think I have a much better grasp overall of the curriculum because planning for three years really makes you figure it out. Now after the second year, we know what we've taught, so we know exactly what's left to teach in the third year of the cycle. . . . Before, with the one-year time slot, I always felt like I was racing at the end because of all the things I was supposed to have taught but didn't have time to teach. But this year I feel a lot less pressure.

"My workload this year is not any more than it was in a traditional classroom."

Kelly Best: "What stands out for me now is that multiage doesn't feel like anything different; it just feels normal. . . .

"What I've discovered this year is that I care more about the kids. I'm more motivated to do my work because I'm more interested in them. There's such a strong relationship. And I'm more personal with their parents. I'll say things that I probably wouldn't have said before, but now I'm comfortable—and so are the parents. I've found that this even transfers to the parents of the first-year students. . . . It's taught me to be more open with parents. When I had students for one year, it was all kind of on the surface when I talked with parents. But they usually want to hear not the diplomatic way, but the straight talk.

"My workload is more than when I had single grade. I've opened up the curriculum, and the more open, the more freedom students have, the more they are writing. They have a language log where they record what they do in language every day. And they have a math log. . . . So I'm reading their logs on a regular basis, which I didn't need to do before. But it doesn't bother me, I think mostly because it's interesting to see what they're learning and I feel good to know that they're being accountable—and I'm being accountable."

Tom LaFerriere: "It's really the depth of relationships that gets to me. . . . At the end of last year, when the sixth graders left, it seemed natural to me. Now that we have broken into this new level of long-term relationship, it seems unusual for me to think that these kids who are now at the end of sixth grade will actually leave. And I can imagine next year, after three years in the room, I'll be petitioning the kids to stay. . . .

"I don't know that I'm working harder than I used to. It's different. In some ways, I'm certainly working more methodically than I used to."

Ginny Semler: "It seems to me that multiage is easier for the children, because they know what's going to happen next year. Only the third-year students have this apprehension about next year. . . .

"It's so interesting to watch the kids grow. You see this not only academically, but also physically and socially. You see all these things that you don't get to see as a one-year teacher. . . .

"The work isn't getting any less. But then, we keep changing things, and every time you change something, there's more work that comes with it. And our projects always seem to end up being ambitious, because we have so many ideas we want to try. . . . Yeah, the work is manageable. And we're used to it.

"The only bad thing is that [my husband] has accepted a job in [another district]. So I'm seeking employment nearer to there. So that's the sad part of this, which is not completing the three-year cycle. I'd like to finish what we started, so leaving will be particularly hard.

"What I'd tell other teachers is this: Multiage is manageable, it's joyous, it's very rewarding."

Dave Matheny: "With the parents, our relationships have become so much stronger. We aren't dancing around the issue like we used to sometimes. When things need to be said on either side, we tend to be more candid, more reliant on the history we share. . . .

"Last year we set up all of these systems in the classroom. And this year we've been fine-tuning them mostly. . . . Materials are still a big issue. We're still working on getting enough books and stuff for the range of kids. . . .

"The amount of time and energy needed has been less this year than the first year. I hope it lessens even more during the third year."

Vicki Voorhees: "I feel really good about how we've developed our program and how our kids have learned. I see a tremendous amount of growth. . . . I see more support from parents because now they know what multiage is, and they want to place their younger children in our class, too.

We have three sets of siblings in our room now. I was uneasy at first, but it's worked out really well. . . .

"When we started last year, I worried some about [whether] the sameness [would] bother kids over time: same teachers, same routines, and so on. But this continuity seems to be the thing that encourages kids to use the freedom we give them, to try things out because they know they're safe. They know that when they're trying something, if it doesn't work out, they can redo it and improve it. So they're not bored at all. The sameness is a sort of safety net for them. . . .

"I've worked the same amount as I did before multiage, or maybe even a little less now. But I'm working in a different way. I'm doing a lot of pre-planning work and getting ready for the lessons and the activities. But at the end of the lessons and activities, there's a lot less to do, because we've turned a lot of the evaluation over to students. And that's the opposite of what I did in a traditional classroom. The kids have their rubrics, they have their techniques [for assessment], so we're looking more at their doing self-evaluating."

NOVEMBER, THIRD YEAR

Of the seven teachers who had completed their second year in multiage classrooms during year two, five returned for their third year. One moved to teach in a different district. One went on parenting leave. The two teachers who had started up their teamed multiage program during the previous year returned for a second year of multiage teaching, as did the teacher who had started a new multiage class in the second year after disbanding her teamed multiage class from the first year. And her teaching partner from the first year, who taught a single-grade class during the second year, started a new multiage class this fall.

The following comments are from the five teachers in their third year of multiage teaching.

"We're off to a great start this fall. We have sixty kids, which is a few less than last year, but this time we were ready for it. We've had sixteen of these kids for three years, and thirty are new. There's lots of fourth graders, and then we've had kids move out of the district and kids move in. . . . We also moved five students out. One was a parent request. We started the other four kids out [of the multiage classroom] with a talk with their parents. We didn't see any of them as having a good chance for success in our class after a year with us. . . . And that was a lot, because the first year we only moved one student out. But all the kids who'd been with us for two years who are in the school came back."

"Teaching children for one year is important—but for three years, you'd better be good!"

"Our students are working together now on projects and taking leadership roles—it's really gone to a level beyond what I expected."

"I do wonder if the kids [who are now in the class for a third year] are exclusive at times. I'm still getting a feel for this. . . . We asked the kids [last June], 'How can we make September work?' And they came up with several ideas, including a mentor–mentee system for new kids. That helped a lot."

"This year has been a lot of fun for me because the relationships are much deeper. I'm seeing the kids growing, and I'm growing myself as a teacher. It's still an awful lot of work."

"With three years, I've seen these kids flower. They're feeling safe, they know you're not just passing through, they know you're sincere, and they really come into being their own persons and finding their abilities."

"We have sixty students this year, with forty back from last year. It's worked out just right for once. . . . This year we had the old students teach the new students about the class routines and procedures and rules. And they did a better job than either one of us, because they told them all the ins and outs and showed them all the forms and everything. And we just sat back and watched. In one day, all of the introductory stuff was done."

"We keep coming up with new systems for the workload that make it easier for us. We go, 'Oh, we should have thought of that two years ago.' But I don't think it would have been possible then. You have to have the experience to see what else to do. The kids come up with ideas, too. They figure out ways to make things work better in the classroom."

"It's really nice to have the time to focus on the new kids and their parents. I got to know them so much sooner."

"We have six sets of siblings this year. These parents were really motivated to get their younger kids into our class."

"We're on a first-name basis with all the returning parents. They trust us. They support us 100 percent and work with us."

"We have ten centers, and kids go in a group from one to the next without choices. That's what we had to do when we went to sixty-four kids last year. Now we're working on giving some choices to kids, but with a safety net so we know what they're doing. We want to put more into their hands."

"We had one girl who was doing well in fifth grade, but she'd only do what she had to. Her parents talked with us, and we agreed to take her in for one year. Now she sees kids of different ages working at different levels, and some of them are working beyond her at seventh-, eighth-grade levels—and in a few weeks, she got it, that she could do a lot more if she tried. She's just taken off here."

"I'm very attached to these kids now after three years. It's a very motherly feeling, protective."

"They're better prepared for junior high than our kids used to be. They're much more flexible."

"We have forty-four kids this year [in a 1/2/3 class]. That's back in the sanity range."

"The kids who have come back to us in the second year are academically far beyond where my second graders used to be. They're doing long division and reading novels. And their writing is advanced."

JUNE, THIRD YEAR

Sharon Tankersley: "I wouldn't want to go back to traditional teaching, ever. I've done a much better job of teaching here, for one thing, because I've had a longer time to work with the curriculum. There's so much continuity in our curriculum from one year to the next. . . . I know the students and their families so much better than I used to. And I believe that we've made some wonderful progress with our special needs kids in particular. . . .

"Cooperative learning has become an integral part of our classroom rather than an extra or an add-on, as it was before. It's just a natural way to do things in multiage. There's also a lot more of kids teaching each other. We do at least one project each trimester that kids do with their families. They're the expert, and they teach other kids about it. And there have been very few presentations where we don't learn something as well as the kids. . . .

"The students are involved in our decision making. In a way, we collaborate with them as well as with each other. They have a lot of input into what curriculum we cover, because with three years, we don't have to rush through things. We have time for what they want to learn in addition to what's required. . . .

"It's going to be very difficult to say good-bye after three years. There's going to be a lot of tears, I think. . . .

"For the third-year students, we've saved some of their work from the first year. We've looked at it with them—'This was when you started, and this is what you can do now.' And it's pretty amazing to see the growth—amazing for the kids and for us, too. . . .

"Oh, yeah, we still change things in the program. I think it will always evolve. It will evolve with the changing kids."

Tom LaFerriere: "I've found it so very rewarding to work with students over the longer period of time. It's given me a different sense of patience with them and a new sense of expectations. It's this ability to set standards for kids over time—that by this point later in the year or next year, I want them to get to a certain point in terms of math or penmanship or whatever. . . .

"I really like the experience of kids taking on different roles as they move through the three years. Sometimes it's been hard not to rush that, so I've had to work on that. . . .

"We've used a lot of ability groups where the kids do self-leveling. And the groups are fluid. Kids can choose to move up or down. This year we've had some fourth graders who wanted to do the hardest problems. And I had to coach them by saying, 'I want to encourage you to try, but don't feel that you've got to be in the toughest group right away.' . . .

"We're still focused on the curriculum, yes; but we see it in terms of each child's context rather than just checking off the objective that we used to teach to the whole class. . . .

"There's a lot of collaboration in our classroom. It's mostly voluntary, and that helps to make it work so well. . . .

"In multiage, nothing is static. Kids are less capable not because there's something wrong with them, but because they're younger or they're just not ready for something yet. They're not slow. But I like this sense that they can really all learn what we need them to learn with the time we have to work with them. . . .

"I'm still not relating directly to the fact that these third-year kids are leaving us. I've said good-bye to so many kids in a twenty-year career, but I've never had these kind of relationships before. . . .

"Oh, we're constantly in change. So, no, we wouldn't say that we've figured it out."

Dave Matheny: "The core of multiage is the strength of relationship with
the kids, the openness of relationship. And after three years, the kids are
quick to say, 'I don't understand this and I want to understand and I know
you can help me so let's get going.' There's an efficiency in that, because
there's no defensiveness about trying to hide what you don't know, which
is so common in our culture. . . .

"We continue to develop open-ended, integrated sorts of projects so
kids can go at them successfully from different skill levels. . . .

"I'm probably more in denial right now about this being the end of the
year. . . . I think in some respects that I feel more parental—they're 'my
kids' much more than they used to be in single-grade [classes]. . . .

"For us, the change and the fine-tuning are a constant."

Vicki Voorhees: "More and more, we've moved away from teaching to the
middle. More and more, it's about meeting the needs of kids as individuals and empowering them with their own learning. . . .

"It's much more being a guide and a resource, getting everything together in the room and setting it up in such a way that they can discover
what you want them to learn through the materials and the environment.
. . .

"We do a lot of grouping, and the groups are flexible and they change
on a regular basis. . . .

"We started three years ago by wanting to build our kids' collaborative
skills. That was our intention. And I think through the years—we've
learned to build lessons and activities where we built in the cooperative
learning. We're using it wisely now, and we're certainly using more collaboration than when we started. . . .

"We still work hard, but we set up, we plan, we provide all the stuff.
We're still teaching, but it's in a guiding sense. We really don't run the
classroom. I think both of us could vanish for some time and our classroom would run itself."

Debbie Snowden: "I'm much more a leader, a guide with them, much less
like I'm in charge. It's more that I'm in charge of the learning environment that allows kids to do what they need to do, and they're in charge of
their learning. . . .

"The emotional tie is much greater after three years, with us and the
kids and among the kids, too. . . .

"The kids learn who can help them. They learn, 'Well, this is a good person who can help me with math.' And when they need help, they get up

and they find that person. In my old class, they'd be in their seats and that couldn't happen. Now it's very much a part of what goes on every day. . . .

"I think if we stop changing, we stop growing, and then we'd become a stagnant program. So we keep changing."

Toward the end of her final interview, Debbie Snowden offered a significant lesson for new multiage teachers: "The key for developing [a] multiage [program] is to go slowly. We take each step at a time. We started out with what we called 'controlled free choice,' where it seemed like kids had a lot of choices, but we were still really in control. And we just slowly kept on letting go of our control. But we needed to ease into it over a couple of years. Because we needed to grow into it as teachers."

⓭

MULTIAGE CLASSROOMS IN THE TWENTY-FIRST CENTURY

It's a warm evening in June. The sun sends long shadows and soft light across the crowd gathered in Burnham Hall, a wonderful old building donated to the town by one of Lincoln's patriarchs. Fifth-grade band members, sitting on wooden chairs in the back of the hall, receive the signal to lift their instruments and begin a steady rendition of "Pomp and Circumstance." Parents, community members, and teachers rise and look back expectantly, watching with broad smiles and moist eyes as twenty-one sixth graders enter the hall one by one, march ceremoniously down the aisle, pass through an elaborately decorated arch, and climb the stairs to the stage, seating themselves in unison following the final sustained chord.

After opening remarks, it's time for student speeches, a highlight of the evening. Each presenter stands at the podium, clear-spoken and confident, surrounded by huge bouquets of spring flowers and an audience that cherishes every word. The ensuing speeches reveal a range of personal reflections from a group of twelve-year-olds at their elementary school promotion ceremony. Students speak of their classroom members as a family, recalling humorous and exciting moments, frustrations and challenges, creative accomplishments, and significant relationships.

One student's message is particularly poignant. A shy insightful girl, Willa brings us into her educational journey thus far: "As I think back on my time at Lincoln Community School, I am struck by how much I've grown here. I have not only developed as a student, but also as an individual with a much stronger sense of who I am and of what is important to me. Over the past seven years, I have found and heard this 'inner voice' with the help of both my teachers and my friends."

A talented artist, writer, and performer, Willa notes that her opportunities to develop these abilities at school were a key to hearing that inner voice. She predicts that her increased confidence, along with this deep sense of self, will guide her well in the next phase of her life.

I find it no coincidence that Willa, along with her articulate classmates, spent the last four years in elementary school in multiage classrooms. Here their talents were acknowledged, nurtured, and honed. And they learned to act as engaged, responsible members of a community, becoming vocal participants in the classroom culture, confident enough to reveal their inner selves to a large audience.

Willa's message is both personal and universal. The struggle to uphold standards of excellence for all children will succeed only if we find a way to honor the inner voice of every child, creating personalized opportunities for growth and challenge. Classrooms where each individual is valued and where children experience different roles over time, and thus learn to look at situations from a variety of perspectives, provide fertile soil for the growth of future community leaders who will be sensitive to the needs of every citizen. Creative thinkers able to collaborate on solving as-yet-unknown challenges of the future will develop in classroom communities where students feel a sense of belonging and ownership, along with the freedom to make their own choices, ask their own questions, and reach high within their own frames of development. These are the greatest benefits of multiage classrooms, as exemplified by Willa's words.

Multiage classrooms offer environments in which students feel both safe and challenged, a sense of belonging as well as the opportunity to change, a place to become a contributing member of a community over at least two successive classroom "generations" and a place where students can leave an imprint that will be carried forward by the "younger generation." What better place to nurture global, American citizens of the future than a multiage classroom?

INDEX

ABOUT THE AUTHORS

Alice Leeds is a 5th/6th grade teacher at Lincoln Community School in Lincoln, Vermont. She has spent twenty years teaching in multiage primary and intermediate classrooms in New York, North Carolina, and Vermont. She has also taught writing and literature classes at the college level. The connections between creativity and learning have always fascinated her.

David Marshak is an associate professor in the School of Education at Seattle University and teaches primarily in the Master in Teaching Program. Marshak has taught in public high school, helped to found and operate an alternative school, served as an assistant superintendent in a public school district, and worked as a consultant with schools in twenty-seven states and provinces. Since 1988, Marshak has both helped to initiate and support multiage classrooms and conducted research about teaching and learning in multiage classrooms.